ALL BLUES

for

JAZZ GUITAR

comping styles, chords
& grooves

By Jim Ferguson

Published by:
Guitar Master Class
Box 551
Santa Cruz, CA 95061-0551
www.fergusonguitar.com

Exclusively distributed by Mel Bay Publications, Inc.

ISBN 0-7866-3128-7

Graphics and layout by GMCP
Photography by Matt Reilley
Hands: Larry Allen
Cover guitar: 1963 Gibson L5-CES

First Printing 1997
Second Printing 1998, revised
Third Printing 1999, revised
Fourth Printing 2001, revised
Fifth Printing 2003

CREDITS

Without the support of the following individuals, this book would have been much more difficult to produce than it was: Howard Morgen, Ole Halen, Dean Kamei, Jon Sievert, Tom Mulhern, Mark Hanson, Rick Gartner, Mark Lang, Marc Smith, and Deborah Roberti. Thanks.

The recording was mixed by Dave Egan at Pine Forest Studio, located in Aptos, California.

CONTENTS

INTRODUCTION

While blues plays an important role in jazz improvisation, guitar educational materials have generally given this fact very little attention as they focus on standard fare such as transcribed solos and familiar scales, modes, chords, and theoretical ideas. But if you come to grips with the ways jazz players approach the blues, then you'll have taken a major step toward becoming fluent with jazz overall, including standards, bebop classics, modal tunes, and bossa novas.

So while other guitar books have addressed blues only sporadically and superficially, this volume—and its companion, *All Blues Soloing For Jazz Guitar: Scales, Licks, Concepts & Choruses*—offers a unique in-depth treatment. Here you'll find authentic straight-four rhythm playing in the style of Freddie Green and others, ensemble-oriented horn-section/piano comping in a variety of styles, and a step-by-step explanation of how to play walking bass lines and chords at the same time. Everything is designed to help you play in a spectrum of settings—from a full big band to a small group to a solo context.

Throughout, the material is clearly presented and gradually introduced, but nothing is sanitized or watered down. Hip chords, progressions, and concepts are abundant. Every example is rhythmically notated—a critical aspect that is conspicuously, and inexplicably, absent from the bulk of chord-oriented jazz guitar instructional materials, especially given that rhythm represents perhaps the single-most important element of creative jazz improvisation. And tablature, which jazz guitar books have also typically avoided, is included. Feel free to start at any point, although working from the beginning will ensure that no idea is missed.

This book stems from years of playing, listening to, and writing about jazz guitar. It also results from knowing—and in some cases having close relationships with—many of the instrument's greatest players. It's dedicated to George Barnes and Red Varner, who taught me a lot about rhythm guitar, as well as blues masters Kenny Burrell, Grant Green, Herb Ellis, Jim Hall, George Benson, Phil Upchurch, Charlie Christian, Barney Kessel, Wes Montgomery, Lenny Breau, and Joe Pass. It was both a challenge and a pleasure to write. I hope you enjoy working and learning from it.

Jim Ferguson
Santa Cruz, California, 1997

ABOUT THE NOTATION, CHORD SYMBOLS & FINGERING

Like fake book lead sheets and many jazz scores, this book uses a combination of standard notation and chord symbols. Consequently, contradictions may occasionally occur between the way in which the music is notated (with simplicity and common practice in mind) and the spelling suggested by a chord symbol. Although an attempt has been made to minimize these enharmonic discrepancies, they are common to jazz notation and frequently unavoidable.

The chord symbols have been notated as simply as possible in most cases. Therefore, chords that could be indicated in more than one way usually reflect the simpler of the two alternatives. In the very few instances where a harmonic structure features three alterations, the umbrella term "alt" (short for "altered") has been used in favor of identifying every tone. Since symbols in general do not represent every component of a given chord, careful analysis is required for complete understanding.

Regarding the standard notation, circled numbers that indicate the string a note is to be played on are valid until a new circled number appears. Throughout this book, only the lowest note of a chord is assigned a circled string number; the strings that the remaining notes are to be played on should be obvious. Moreover, fingering is given for a chord or passage only the first time it appears in the music. And courtesy accidentals are included whenever a note in a different octave is unaffected by a sharp or flat, and when a note in the first beat of a new measure reverts to the key signature at hand.

Rhythms should be interpreted with a swing eighths feel. Therefore, what appears as a pair of straight eighth-notes should be read as a triplet quarter-note followed by a triplet eighth. Articulations are included to clarify certain passages and rhythms; however, they often represent only one option and should be freely explored and experimented with.

Finally, the diagrams and tablature, common to so many guitar-oriented publications, feature very few special symbols. For that reason, a comprehensive key has not been provided. Consult the accompanying text and the Glossary for more information.

1 12-BAR BLUES PROGRESSIONS

Before exploring the specific elements of comping approaches, it is constructive to understand the range of blues progressions used in jazz. While blues melodic ideas can be applied in varying degrees to virtually any tune, the purest blues song form is 12-bars long.

From Swing To Bop

This book focuses on the following basic progression, which is common to both swing and bebop. (As with all progressions in this section, the Roman numeral notation indicates *basic* root movements and chord qualities only; there are many possible interpretations and variations. In other words, progressions in Roman numeral form only represent harmonic skeletons.)

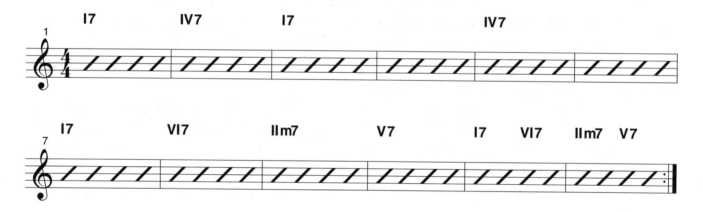

It can be embellished with substitute and passing chords in many ways; the next example represents just one possibility.

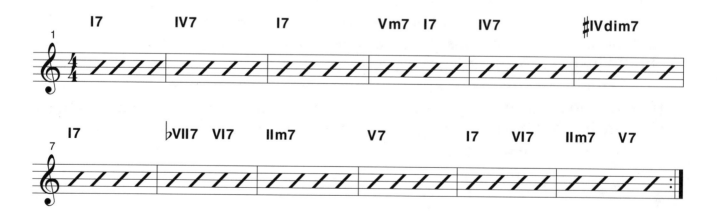

Blues Roots

The 12-bar structure's exact origin is unknown; however, it probably reaches back to the late 1800s. Regardless, it comprises three four-bar phrases (discussed in more detail in Chapter 3). The next two patterns show two of the earliest and simplest progressions. The first example is identified with early jazz, while the second is linked to purer, more down-home blues styles; however, remember that these associations are not mutually exclusive. While in both cases the IV7 chord is indicated in measure 2, it is common for the first four bars to feature only the tonic chord (I7; again, certain chord qualities are variable).

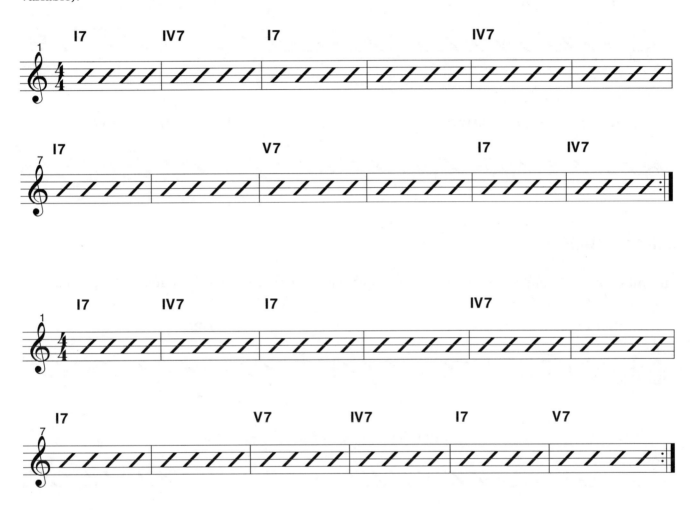

Modern I-IV-V

This next variation is associated with modern arrangers such as Thad Jones. It is based on the down-home version of the blues but features a more sophisticated turnaround.

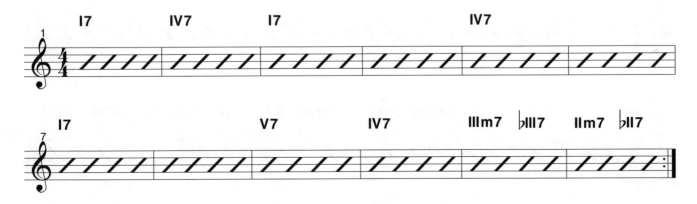

T-Bone's 12-Bar Blues

A common offshoot of the swing/bebop blues worth mentioning is the "Stormy Monday" progression, so called because it is the basis of the well-known tune by T-Bone Walker. It's usually taken at a relatively slow tempo.

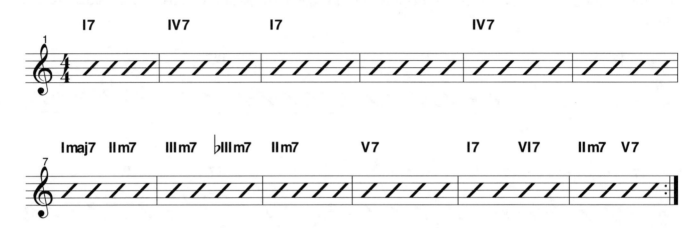

Minor Blues

In a minor key, 12-bar progressions used in mainstream jazz include these variants (the first is basic, the second more elaborate):

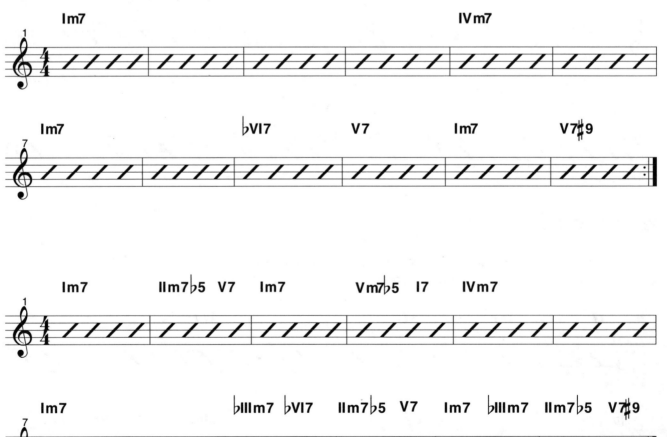

New York Changes

This pattern utilizes what is sometimes referred to as "New York changes," "cycle blues," "II-V blues," or "'Confirmation' blues, because it utilizes changes similar to those of the Charlie Parker tune of the same name. ("Confirmation" isn't a 12-bar blues; one example of how Parker used this progression in a 12-bar context is "Blues For Alice.")

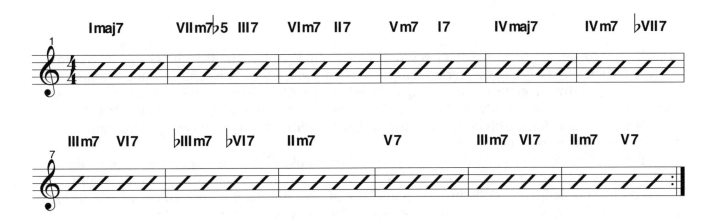

The swing/bebop progression forms the basic harmonic skeleton for many tunes, including ones written by Charlie Parker ("Now's The Time," "Billie's Bounce," "Bloomdido," "Relaxin' At Camarillo," "Cool Blues"), Barney Kessel ("Swedish Pastry"), Sonny Rollins ("Tenor Madness," "Blues For Philly Joe"), and many others. It is also frequently applied to 12-bar tunes not originally written for this specific sequence, such as Duke Ellington's "C Jam Blues" and "Things Ain't What They Used To Be" and John Coltrane's "Trane's Blues." Many artists wouldn't consider a set or an album complete without including at least one blues, a process that has resulted in innumerable originals by players who didn't or don't normally consider themselves composers.

While the overwhelming variations in terms of chord voicings, inversions, and substitutions preclude touching on every possibility, within these pages you'll find a wealth of professional practices, including hip devices, voicings, connections, and rhythmic phrases. Each will be discussed as it arises. Feel free to open this book to any point; however, it is highly recommend that you work from the beginning so that a detail introduced in one context is not overlooked when it is applied to another. Starting now, make it your goal to transfer these ideas to every key—especially those most commonly used in jazz: C, E♭, F, G, A♭, B♭, and even D♭ and G♭.

2 IN THE TRADITION— STRAIGHT-FOUR RHYTHM

Straight four-to-the-bar rhythm playing is synonymous with Freddie "Mr. Rhythm" Green, who held the guitar chair with Count Basie's various large and small groups for a half century. But there were many other fine rhythm guitarists, including George Van Eps, Allan Reuss, Carl Kress, George Barnes, Steve Jordan, and, more recently, Bucky Pizzarelli, Wayne Wright, Jim Hall, and Herb Ellis. To a degree, this style is also associated with both western and Django Reinhardt-inspired Gypsy swing, and it can even be applied to purer blues forms.

Although this approach to rhythm playing is often overlooked by players interested in more modern jazz styles, any guitarist who aspires to increase his or her ability to play jazz can gain a wealth of highly useful knowledge and skills, including solid rhythmic acuity, familiarity with the inner workings of the fingerboard, and an awareness of voice-leading (the movement of individual notes, or voices). Essential in a big band context, it can also be used in small-group settings and even combined with the piano/horn section-type comping addressed in Chapter 3.

"Fat Chords"

The traditional Freddie Green-forged type of rhythm work primarily employs three-note open-voiced chords played on strings six, four, and three, although chords with more notes can occasionally be used. George Barnes referred to three-note voicings as "fat chords," due to their full sound, a by-product of the wide interval, often a tenth, between their outer voices. Most three-note chords are easy to finger and can be grabbed quickly; however, becoming fluent with them can be a thorny proposition, especially if your knowledge of the fingerboard isn't what it could be. The difficulties are three-fold:

1. The qualities of three-note chords generally encompass the four triads (major, minor, augmented, and diminished), as well as 6th, 7th, minor 7th, major 7th, diminished 7th, and a few miscellaneous chords, such as 9th and minor/major7th. Chords beyond the triad necessitate that one or more notes be omitted, and when the root (tonic) is left out, a structure can be tricky to locate on the fingerboard due to the absence of common reference points.

2. This leads to a phenomenon that is both a difficulty and an advantage: Chords in general, and many three-note chords in particular, can be applied to more than one harmonic context. In other words, they have more than one name—and are sometimes referred to as "chord synonyms"—and can be used for a variety of purposes, which can be confusing initially.

3. This final point is less of a difficulty and can be easily learned: Since most three-note chords are in open voicing, a string (usually the 5th) must be skipped and damped, or muffled. To do this, touch the unwanted string with part of your finger positioned on the next lower string.

Fortunately, three-note chords (and many others) can be systematized to a certain extent and grouped in ways that facilitate not only their memorization, but also their location on the fingerboard. Before we begin to take a look at some of these methods, familiarize yourself with the following G major triads in root position, first inversion, and second inversion, respectively (G is used so the chords can be presented in order, starting with root position):

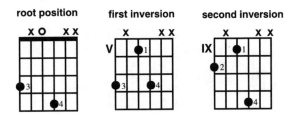

Chromatically raising the 5th of a root-position triad transforms the G major triad into the following (sometimes it is useful to finger the 5th of the root-position major triad on the fifth string):

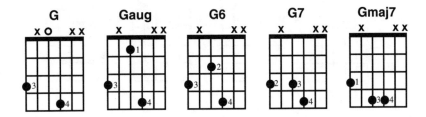

Other chords associated with this position include:

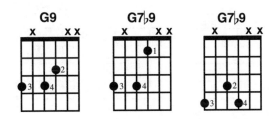

Lowering the 3rd of a root-position major triad results in a root-position minor triad. If you then chromatically raise its 5th, you produce:

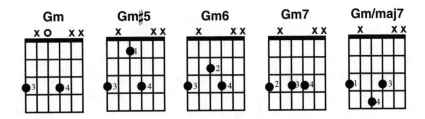

The first-inversion G major triad is less flexible (for instance, apart from Gaug, chromatically raising its 5th in the preceding manner produces fingerings that are rarely used). Here are the most common chords associated with this position:

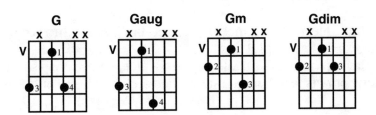

Chromatically lowering the root of second-inversion G major generates these commonly used chords:

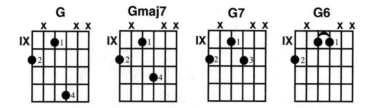

Beginning with a second-inversion minor triad and then chromatically lowering the root produces these:

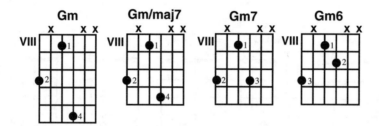

Finally, we have these miscellaneous items (Gaug is produced by raising the 5th of the second-inversion G major triad; G7♭5 and G7♯5 arise from respectively lowering and raising the 5th of G7):

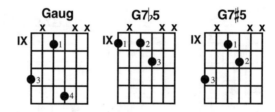

Observe that some of the preceding chords shown in diagram form share the same physical shape. While a thorough study of chord synonyms is beyond the scope of this book, begin to think of these as having more than one letter name. For instance, root-position Gm6 in three-note form (G-E-B♭, from low to high) can be viewed and used as Gdim7 (no 5th), C7 (no root), F♯7♭9 (no root, no 5th), and Em7♭5 (no root, no 7th).

Many of the preceding chords are used in the music to come. While some of their shapes suggest only one practical fingering, others can be played in more than one way. When you begin to apply them to actual progressions and thread them together, look for places where the same finger can be used for more than one chord in succession. This device, known as the "guide finger," can enable you to change chords smoothly and quickly with little effort. With three-note chords, guides usually involve the third string and fingers 3 or 4. Before we begin looking at some complete 12-bar examples, however, two other topics merit consideration.

Articulation, Attack, Swing

The sound and rhythmic feel of traditional four-to-the-bar jazz rhythm is critical. While extensive listening is essential, here are a few helpful tips.

Authentic rhythm playing can only be achieved with a pick, whose crisp sound is unobtainable with any other method. (Many purists feel that an unamplified arch-top is the only possibility, although you can get a surprisingly good sound on an electric hollowbody, and even a solidbody). If you play finger-style, use your thumb , although even the longest, strongest nail falls short of the pick's clarity.

A variety of articulations are possible depending on a tune's tempo, and the exact nature of the articulations involved is subject to debate. Of the tunes that are most appropriate for a straight rhythm approach, the majority are taken at tempos ranging from medium ($\quarternote$=116) to brisk ($\quarternote$=184) swing. By in large, every example in this chapter, should be treated like so, which emphasizes beats two and four, commonly referred to as the back beat or after beat):

Notice that the included articulations indicate that beats 1 and 3 are played as a full quarter-note, while two and four are slightly accented and detached so that the quarter-note is closer to equaling a dotted-eighth (this can be achieved with left-hand damping by slightly relaxing the finger pressure applied to the strings). At very fast tempos, it is relatively common, and often effective, to play all four beats as being detached. It is also possible to alternate between this articulation and one that emphasizes the back beats; exactly when this is done in the course of a tune depends on the player's discretion. Slow tempos can be realized by either playing the usual articulation, albeit at the slower tempo, or by sustaining the chords as long as possible. All of the preceding articulations can be effective, depending on how they're applied.

In traditional rhythm playing, it is also acceptable to occasionally play upbeats, although overuse of this device can make a piece sound dated and more like Django-inspired Gypsy swing than conventional jazz. Probably the most appropriate point at which to use an upstroke is on the "and" of beat four, right before a chord change (it is common for the left hand to be released on the "and" of four, producing more of a percussive effect than discernable pitches):

Chart Interpretation

Rhythm guitar parts usually reflect one of two extremes. In the first, common to big band scores, a chart's chords are presented in too much detail, the result of attempting to indicate an arrangement's overall harmonic scheme. In this case, the guitar only needs to play the basics. In other words, when faced with changes that include extensions and alterations, simplify them. In most instances, chords usually should be reduced to 7ths and simpler.

Sometimes, however, a chart provides only a harmonic skeleton. In this case, it is usually appropriate to add passing chords, many of which are to be found in the following examples. The key is listening to the bass player, whose stylistic influences will suggest not only the degree to which you can add passing chords, but also indicate their nature. A final bit of advice: To help maintain a cohesive sense of time in the rhythm section, focus your ears on the drummer's hi-hat, which emphasizes beats two and four.

Basic Blues Chord Routes

Rhythm guitar should be fun to play and involve an element of creativity. At the same time, it should fit into the musical surroundings. With a good knowledge of three-note chords and progressions, you should ultimately be able to spontaneously thread together effective, flexible, logical patterns that constitute a kind of rhythm-oriented improvisation. But to do that, you have to start with the basics.

B♭ Blues. This complete 12-bar chorus, in the key of B♭, is the first example of a blues progression played with three-note chords. Only three different fingerings are used for the entire 12 bars:

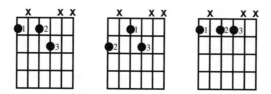

Although this simple treatment utilizes no passing chords, it can be effective if a bit monotonous. Focus on the articulation of your attack, maintaining the proper feel, and developing rock-solid time. Also pay attention to how guide fingers ease moving from one chord to the next. (First, play the initial B♭7 chord with fingers 1, 2 and 3 and limit yourself to using only those fingers for the rest of the piece; notice that your 3rd finger can remain on the third string throughout. Next, use fingers 2, 3, and 4, keeping 4 on the third string throughout.)

TRACK 1

"Twelve For Three"

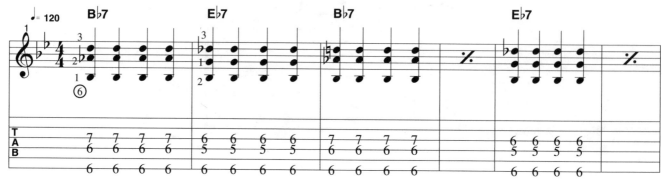

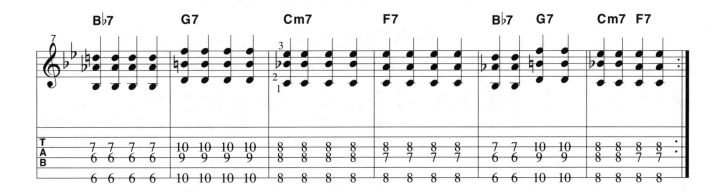

This next pattern begins the same as the preceding one, but takes an alternative route to VI7 (G7). (Note the second-inversion Cm7 in bars 9 and 12.) While three-note chords confined to strings six, four, and three are limited in terms of providing strong starting and ending points for progressions—in this case, a typical blues—there are many ways they can be connected and routed when substitutes and passing chords are added to the equation, as you will soon see. Again, work with more than one fingering and apply the guide concept.

"Blues Basis"

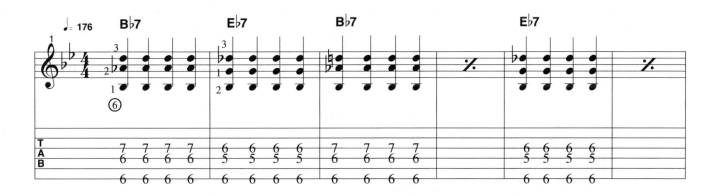

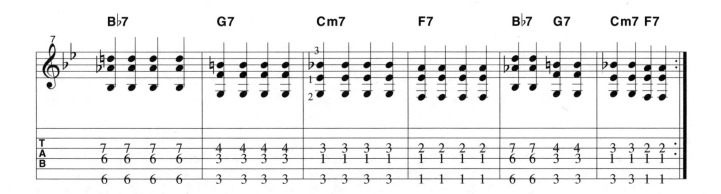

F Blues. This next chorus and pattern introduces the key of F and represents a new fingerboard starting point. (Whereas the previous examples began with a root-position dominant 7th, now you begin with a dominant 7th in second inversion.) Notice how the pattern works its way down to F7 at the first fret; from there, the turnaround ascends, resolving back to second-inversion F7.

"Work Down Blues"

Here's another sequence that begins with second-inversion F7, but this time an alternate route is taken to VI7 (D7):

"Route 2 Blues"

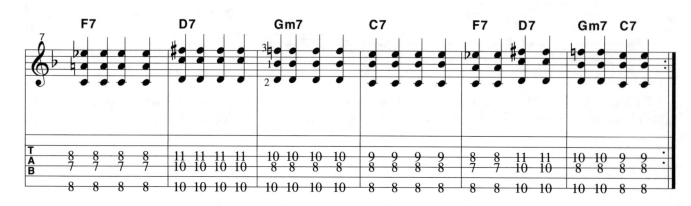

The four preceding 12-bar choruses represent not only two of the most common jazz keys, but also two different starting points on the fingerboard. Memorize these patterns, playing them until they become second nature. Next, begin transposing them to other keys. Although they use very few chords combined, they include enough possibilities to play in every conceivable key.

Voice-Leading

Although a thorough discussion of voice-leading—the relationship between the notes of two successive chords—is beyond the scope of this book—the use of more active patterns that employ common substitutions and passing chords warrants its consideration.

It is possible to construct a rhythm guitar part that sometimes uses relatively wide distances between chords (by jumping up or down the fingerboard); however, for the most part the connections should be smooth and closely related. Fortunately, three-note chords are simple and flexible enough to allow this with relative ease. Depending on where you are on the fingerboard, certain progressions allow you to select inversions that produce voice-leading that is very pleasing—both aesthetically and theoretically. For instance, consider this IIm7-V7-I in the key C major:

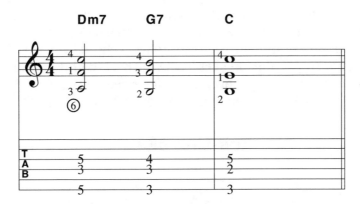

In moving from the second-inversion Dm7 to root-position G7, notice that the outer voices both descend by step—C moves down a half-step as A moves down a whole—while F remains in common to both chords. Next, in moving from root-position G7 to second-inversion C, G remains in common while the upper voices move in contrary motion: F goes down one half-step to E, while B ascends to C. The overall effect is smooth and logical.

When circumstances—including certain harmonic sequences or fingerboard locations—make maintaining smooth connections between every note inconvenient if not impossible, focus your attention on one of two places: either the uppermost voice or the bass. In the next example—a common IV-♯IVdim7-I progression in the key of G—although second-inversion C's lower two voices each skip upward by a minor third interval, the upper voice rises by a half-step in moving to C♯dim7, creating an overall effect that is smooth and logical as it finally connects to I in first inversion:

Equal success can sometimes be had by focusing primarily on the bass voice. Remember that the overall goal is to seamlessly thread your way through a given progression. As you work your way up to using passing chords, remember to generally reserve the strong beats (the first and third) for chords that are directly related to the harmony at hand, using passing chords for the weak beats (the second and fourth). All that having been said, let's now look at some ways of treating a 12-bar blues with chord changes that are more active.

More Active Chordal Patterns

Half-Step Approaches

One of the most effective chordal devices that will help you to seamlessly string together one chord after another is the half-step approach concept. Due to its simplicity, it makes a good place to begin creating chord patterns that are active, although playing more chords isn't required and sometimes isn't appropriate. It does, however, provide more opportunity to sculpt the voice-leading and make a part more interesting.

Bb Blues. Throughout the following 12-bar chorus in Bb, the familiar principal blues chords are approached at strategic times—often on the weak beats— from a half-step above or below. (It's also good to know that when you use a dominant 7th to approach a chord from a half-step above, the dominant 7th is in a b5 relationship to the target chord's V7. This is commonly known as a b5 (or lowered 5th) substitute. Mastering this type of movement is an excellent preliminary step to including other chord devices, many of which are covered in the pages to come.

TRACK 3

"Half-Step Blues"

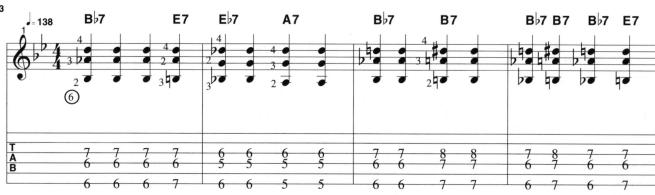

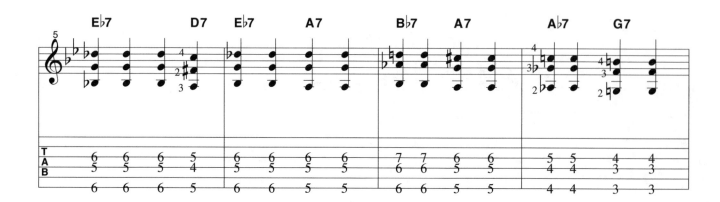

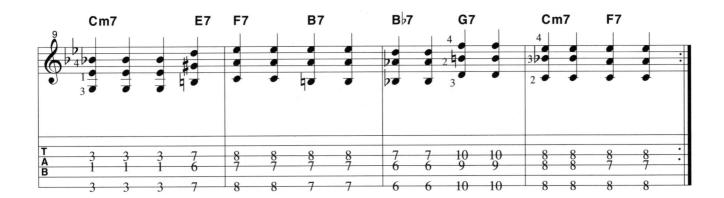

Mixed Concepts

Now let's see how concepts can be combined. The next two examples are devoted to more active patterns in the key of F in that they feature at least two chords per measure. Remember that the use of guide fingers is essential when changing chords so frequently. Furthermore, don't be distracted by the extra chord symbols; frequently, the important aspects are the target, or main, chords, and how you get to them, not the specific names of each little step along the way.

    F Blues. This first 12-bar chorus begins with a quintessential and universally useful swing progression: I-I7-IV6-IVm6-I that can be used for everything from "rhythm changes" to standards like "Honeysuckle Rose" to turnarounds. Particularly notice the use of inversions; second- inversion F and F7 lead to root-position B♭6 and B♭m6, which lead to first-inversion F—very smooth. The progression descends; here's an equivalent inversion-specific ascending sequence—I7-I-IV6-♯IVdim7-I7—that moves up from I7's root:

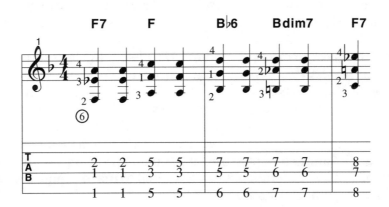

In measure 3, C7 is used as a passing chord (any chord can be preceded by its dominant 7th). Bar 4 features the half-step approach principle. Root-position F7 moves up to first-inversion F, after which A7 approaches B♭7 from a half-step below (try using Faug instead of A7). There are several ways measure 4 could be treated. One is to use this type of harmonized one-chord-per-beat method (since the chord names are open to interpretation, it might be simpler to just think of this as a kind of walking passage based on F7 and leave it at that. (Here the idea is used for I7, but it could be applied to any dominant 7th chord; furthermore, the rhythm can be expanded, a device also known as augmentation, so that you play each chord for two beats, as you'll see later in this chapter.)

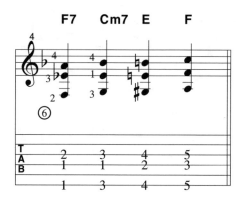

You could also use a passing diminished 7th chord, like so:

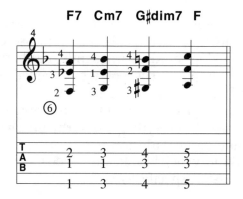

A minor 7th chord can temporarily replace a dominant 7th, as in bar 5 where Fm7 briefly replaces B♭7. Here's the substitution rule: Regardless of a dominant 7th's function in a progression, temporarily think of it as V7; the minor 7th that you want to use in its place would then be its IIm7 chord, whose root name is a perfect fifth above the root name of the dominant 7th. So, for B♭7 (the temporary V7 of E♭), substitute Fm7, IIm7 of E♭.

In measure 6, Bdim7 links B♭7 to F7 (a IV7-♯IVdim7-I7). Ideally, the bass should move from a root-position IV7 chord to root-position ♯IVdim7 to second-inversion I7 as it does here, although this concept can also be used with other inversions. Bars 7 and 8 descend chromatically from F7 to D7, while measure 8's D7♭5 (the equivalent of A♭7) approaches bar 9's Gm7 from a half-step above. Also in bar 9, D♭7 approaches measure 10's C7 from a half-step above, and C7♭5 (essentially the same as F♯7) approaches measure 11's F7 from a half-step above. The turnaround in bars 11 and 12 features no frills, although the concluding C7 requires a leap up the fingerboard for the repeat. In this case the leap is acceptable since what follows is so smooth, but if you wanted to make a more seamless transition back to the beginning, use this ascending turnaround:

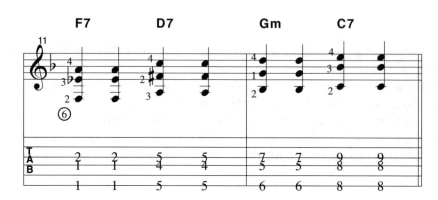

Here's the complete chorus, which should smoothly groove:

"Freddie's Home"

TRACK 4

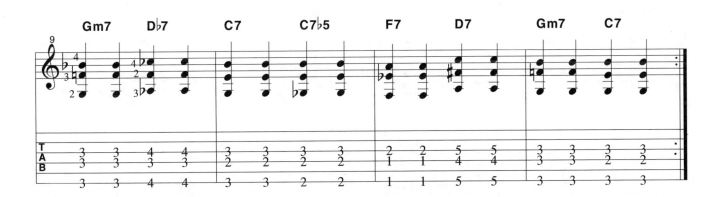

The next 12 begins in the same manner, but heads in a different direction in measure 2, as Bdim7 leads to second-inversion F7. In bar 3, there's another minor 7th substitute, this time for I7. Measure 4's F7b5 (the same as B7) approaches Bb7 from a half-step above. The treatment in bars 5 and 6 should be familiar by now.

Measures 7 and 8 can be viewed in more than one way. As the progression stands, it's a I-IV6-IIIm7-VI7, which is common to bebop (more on this later), and makes for smooth voice-leading. But if you think of Bb6 as Gm, the progression becomes I-IIm-IIIm7, which suggests the "Stormy Monday" sequence. It sounds good, regardless of how you think of it.

In bar 9, a root-position Gm7 is followed by first-inversion Gm and then B7, which approaches C7 from a half-step below. This progression is the minor equivalent of measure 4 in the preceding 12-bar example. Here are a couple of common one-chord-per-beat variations; the first moves to C7 with a half-step approach, while the second uses a passing dim7 chord:

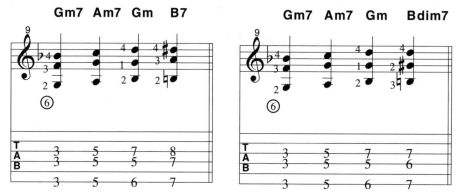

Lastly, measure 9 moves to 10 with a half-step approach, 10 goes to 11 with contrary motion, and the turnaround in 11 and 12 is simple and direct.

"Freddie's Home, Too"

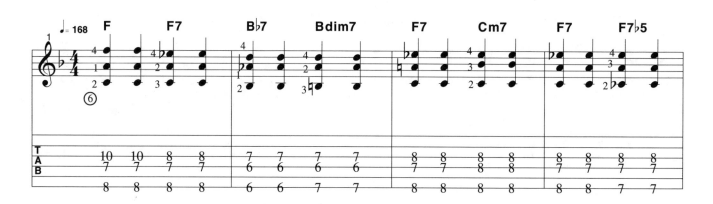

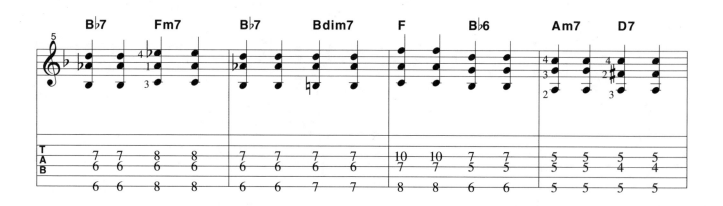

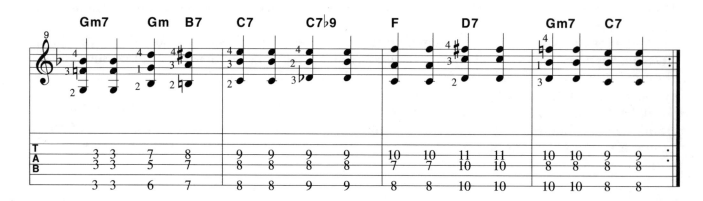

B♭ Blues. Now let's focus on more active patterns in B♭ by considering the upcoming 24-bar example, which uses many of the devices already mentioned. In measure 1 B♭7♭9 (enharmonic to E7) approaches bar 2's E♭7 from a half-step above. Measure 2's E♭m6 (IVm6) is a common linking chord between IV7 and I7. Bars 3 and 4 feature a harmonized bass line. This same type of idea was discussed earlier; each chord now receives two beats.

In measure 5 B♭m7 temporarily substitutes for E♭7, and in bar 6 ♯IVdim7 (Edim7) connects IV7 (E♭7) to I7 (B♭7). I7 (B♭7) chromatically descends to VI7 (G7) in measures 7 and 8. Bars 9 and 10 feature half-step approaches; in bar 9, C7♭9, which is essentially the same as G♭7, approaches measure 10's F7 from a half-step above, while F7♭5 (the same as B7) approaches bar 11's B♭7 in the same way. The turnaround in measures 11 and 12 is treated directly, with the exception of bar 12's A7, which approaches B♭7 from a half-step below.

The second 12-bar chorus features many of these same devices. The first measure of the second chorus (bar 13) features half-step movement, while bar 14 uses ♯IVdim7, discussed earlier, but with four notes, which nicely voice-leads to measure 15's first-inversion B♭. Also in bar 15, Fm7 temporarily replaces B♭7, while measure 16's B♭7♭9 (the same as E7) approaches E♭7 from a half-step above. Bars 17 and 18 employ familiar devices—a minor 7th substitute for a dominant 7th and the ♯IVdim7 chord. Measure 19 features a descending harmonized sequence that uses a passing diminished chord, and in bar 20 G7 is approached from a half-step above and transformed into G7♭9 (the same as D♭7), which essentially approaches measure 21's C7 from a half-step above. Also in bar 21, C7♭5 (the same as F♯7) chromatically approaches measure 22's F7, and Faug voice-leads to measure 23's B♭7. The turnaround in measures 23 and 24 is a bit different from what has been seen so far. The Bdim7 can be viewed from two perspectives: as a passing chord linking I7 to IIm or as a substitute for VI7 (G7♭9). Also, Bdim7 to bar 24's Cm and F7♭5 results in contrary motion, while F7♭5 (the same as B7) approaches B♭7 from a half-step above.

"Stompin' With The Count"

TRACK 5

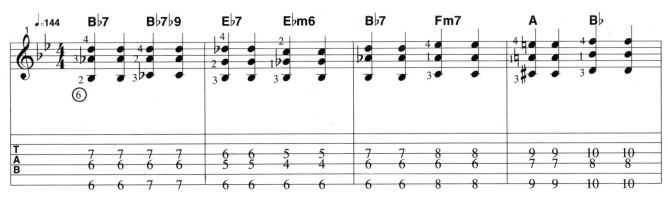

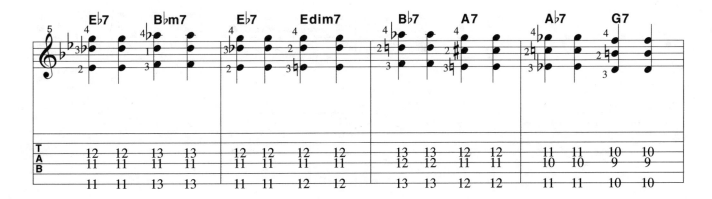

All Blues

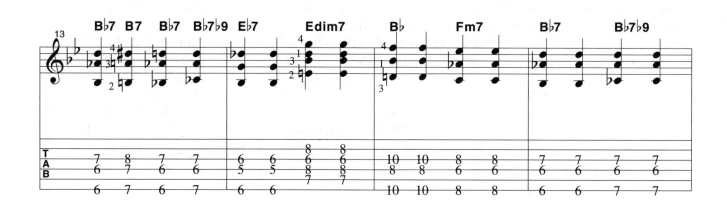

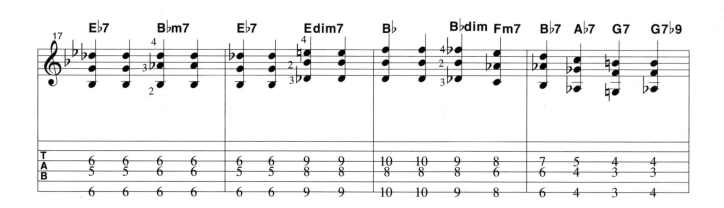

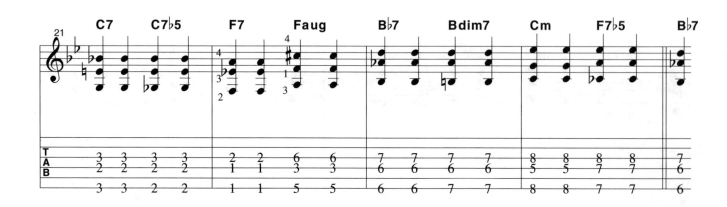

Modern Changes, Traditional Approach

B♭ Blues. While this next example in B♭ features some familiar devices, it also takes routes that are more chromatic and common to bebop. Although measure 1's I6-I7 suggests the swing era, the VIm7-♭VIm7-Vm7-♭V7 sequence in bars 3 and 4 is more bebop-oriented (in measure 3, B♭ could replace Gm7 and C7 could replace G♭7). Bars 5 and 6 include previously discussed devices; however, in bars 7 and 8 the progression again takes a more chromatic turn as it moves from I7 to IV7 to IIIm7 to ♭III7 (a common sub for VI7). In measures 9 and 10, the normal II7 and V7 chords are each preceded by their minor 7th substitutes, creating a series of IIm7-V7s. Finally, the turnaround leaps from B♭6 in bar 11 to D♭7 and then descends, forming a I6-♭III7-II7-♭II7. All in all, a modern treatment in a traditional package.

TRACK 6

"Swinging On The Spot"

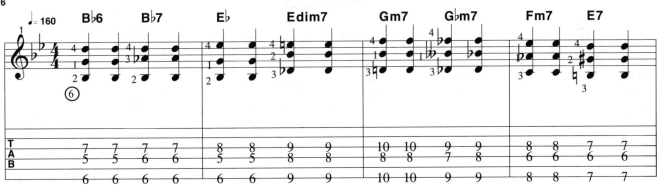

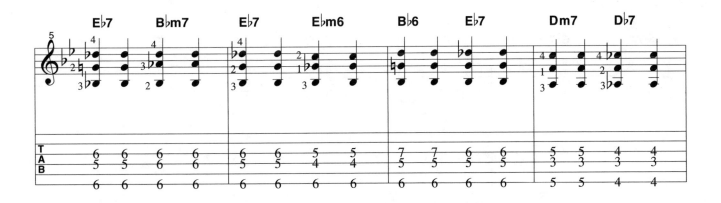

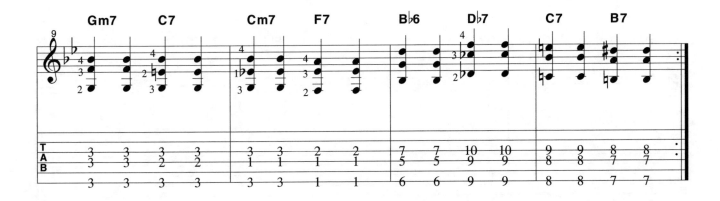

25

2/2 Style

C Blues. Even when playing in groups where your main job is maintaining straight four-to-the-bar underpinning, it may occasionally be appropriate to intersperse choruses of 2/2 (the time signature could also be indicated with the alla breve, or "cut time," symbol). Some bass players particularly like to mix this up with straight four, and when the two feels are factored into an arrangement, the result can be quite effective. This time the key is C, and although this style gravitates toward standard ensemble comping, the use of three-note chords and conservative rhythmic figures keeps things from straying too far afield.

Most of the devices are common. Notice the use of four-note voicings in measures 2 and 3. Bar 4's G♭7 is equivalent to C7♭9 and approaches F7 by a half-step. In measure 5, G♭7 approaches Fm7 by a half-step. (Bar 6's IVm7-♭VII7 is a "back door" method of connecting IV7 to I7.). Bars 7 and 8 move from I7 to IV7 to IIIm7, but instead of going to VI7, IIIm7 chromatically descends to IIm7 via ♭IIIm7. The turn-around leaps from C7 up to E♭7 (equivalent to VI7, or A7), and then descends chromatically to Dm7 and then D♭7). With a metronome clicking on beats two and four, try going back and forth between this chorus with one played in straight four. Also try playing these chords on beats two and four only.

"Two's Blues"

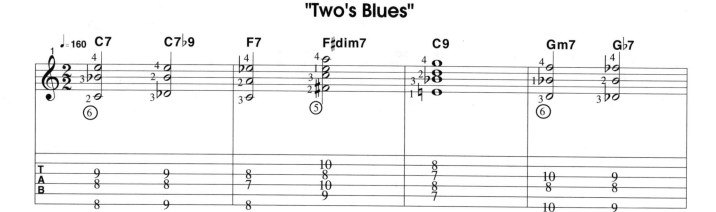

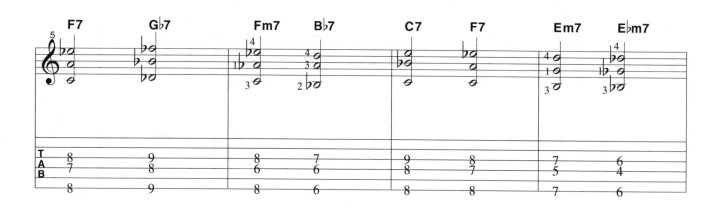

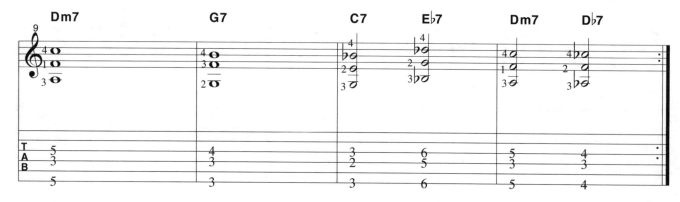

Shuffle Grooves

F Blues. Although the next chorus is based on I7-IV7-V7 blues changes rather than the jazz version, it demonstrates how three-note chords can be used in a more down-home situation. Bars 1 through 3 are a simple variation of a harmonized figure discussed earlier, but without the chromaticism. In measure 3 the idea is carried up one step further before it again descends and approaches Bb7 from a half-step above in measure 5.

In bars 5 and 6 the same type of idea is adapted for Bb7, and then F7 is approached from a half-step above in measure 7. Finally, the turnaround is based upon the universally useful I-I7-IV6-IVm6-I sequence mentioned earlier. In this case, though, it is reduced so that each chord gets one beat, leading things back to F in bar 12. From there, C7 is approached from a half-step above (Db7 could be interpreted as Abdim7), and then another half-step approach takes things back to the top.

Play with a laid-back loping feel, sustaining the chords for as long as possible. Also play each chord twice with a true shuffle swing-eighths feel.

"Slow Funky Shuffle"

TRACK 7

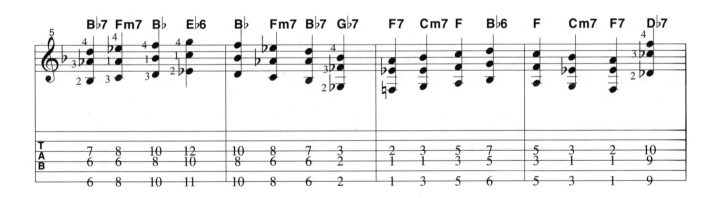

Here are two other turnarounds that could also be plugged into the last two measures (how you get into them is up to you). The first one is similar to the "universal" sequence but uses a I-I7-IV-#IVdim7-I and ascends instead of descends. The second jumps from root-position F7 up to first- inversion F, and then moves down chromatically. Bar 12 has a bluesy down-home flavor and works well when used as the last measure of the "universal" progression:

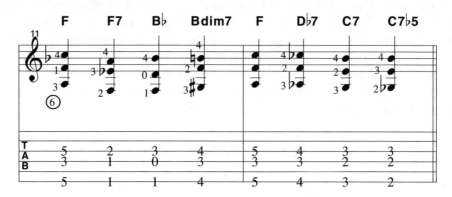

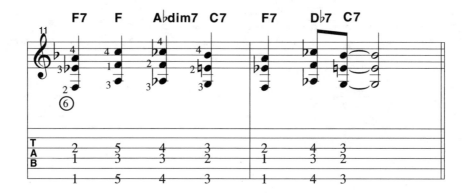

These alternative shuffle-type patterns also work well in a I-IV-V context. There are any number of ways they can be applied to the complete 12-bar form; find some of them on your own. Notice that they're shown in the key of G instead of F (for reasons that should be obvious) and they include elements played on the off beats. Even though other chords are employed, think of the patterns as being centered around I.

The first example uses only major chords, but you could also use G7 instead of G (for the G major chord, try using the alternate fingering that places D on the fifth string). The second uses a half-step approach that brings things back to G7:

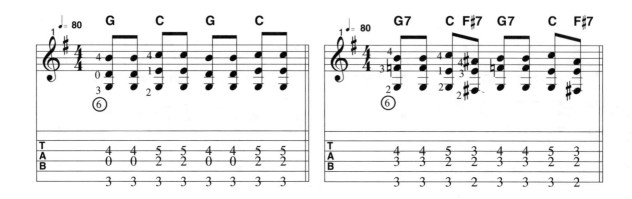

Slow Blues

G Blues. Slower tempos seem to beg for more activity, supplied here by using a chord per beat. Nevertheless, many of these ideas will work well at medium and fast clips. Be sure to transpose elements so you can play them in all keys. Chordal concepts used earlier in this chapter will be described only briefly.

"Herbie's Here" begins at the 3rd fret, walks up through measure 1 and continues with the same idea through measure 2. Bar 3 features the universal I-I7-IV6-IVm6 reduced to one chord per beat, moving down to measure 4's first-inversion G. From there, the sequence takes a somewhat different route than seen before, moving from I to V7 to I7 to ♭V7, which places passing chords on the weak beats.

Walking lines often begin with a root-position chord; however, measure 5 begins with second-inversion. In measure 6, the V7 of IV7 (G7) moves things back to IV7, which in turn heads for I via IV6. These devices have been used earlier, but not in the same manner. Here's an alternative route for measures 3 through 6 that uses a series of half-step approaches involving minor 7th chords, moves down to C7, and then back up where it resolves to bar 7's first-inversion G:

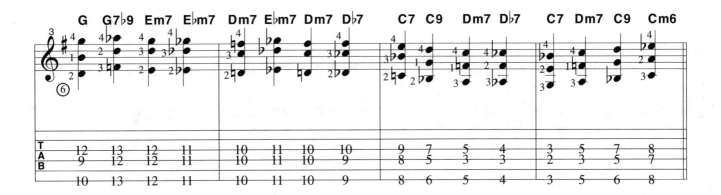

Measure 7 momentarily shifts up from first-inversion G and then back down as it ultimately heads toward VI7 in measure 8, where the fourth-beat B♭m7 approaches Am7 from a half-step above. The low E7 will sound good if you take care to damp the open A string; if you want, also include fifth-string B at the second fret. To avoid going that low altogether, try this alternative route for bar 8, which is just one of many possibilities:

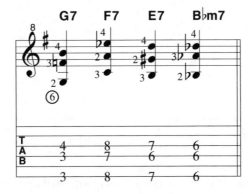

Measure 9 features a nice minor-based walking passage mentioned earlier in the chapter, and smoothly moves to bar 10, which features half-step approaches. The turnaround—one of the most common and best sounding in the jazz guitar vocabulary—also relies on the half-step approach. At the indicated tempo, play the chords as legato (sustained) as possible.

TRACK 8

"Herbie's Here"

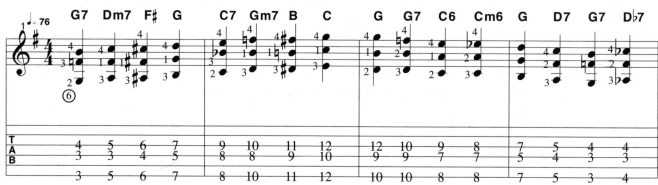

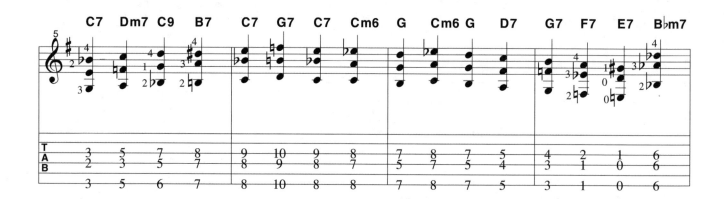

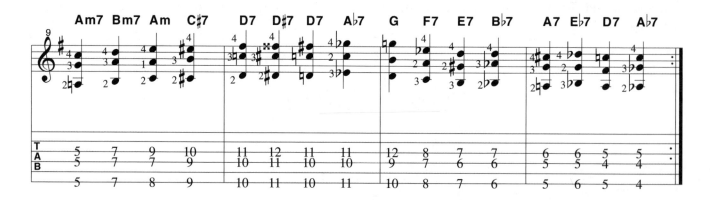

This next example begins in another fingerboard location and again uses some familiar devices. Measure 1 features half-step approaches, while bar 2 walks down from IV7 to I7 (observe the third-inversion C9). The harmonization in measure 3 is similar to one used earlier in the key of F, with the exception of the half-step approaches at the end of bar 4.

Measure 5 moves from second-inversion C7 to root position with another third-inversion 9th chord and a diminished 7th passing chord, while bar 6 features a pattern that has been used many times over. Half-step movements are used in measures 7 and 8 and 11 and 12.

"Walking The Blues"

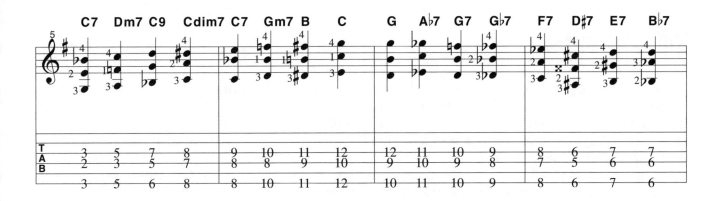

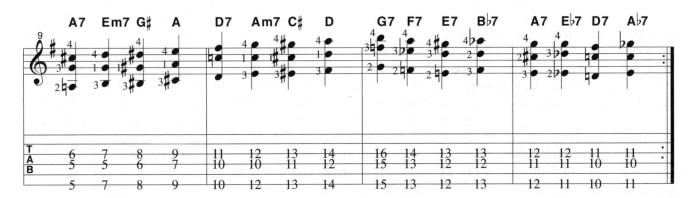

Afterthoughts

Don't forget to transpose these ideas to all keys. Ideally, you should be able to spin out chorus after chorus, regardless of the number of chords you choose to play in each measure. The quantity of the chords isn't the imperative—it's time and tone.

3 SWING TO BOP— SMALL-GROUP COMPING

Freddie Green-style rhythm playing can, of course, be used in a small-group context; however, more modern comping approaches are essentially modeled after either a big or small band horn section or a pianist's left hand. Depending on the music's style, a wide variety of rhythmic approaches are possible—from riffs that repeat over the course of a blues' 12 bars to linear, free-flowing figures with little or no repetition from chorus to chorus. Each has its place and can accommodate a wide variety of chord voicings and harmonic concepts.

Riff Comping

Riff guitar comping is similar to how the big bands of the '30s—led by Bennie Moten, Count Basie, and others—used repeated rhythmic figures for ensemble backgrounds. "Some of the musicians in early black bands couldn't read that great, so they developed riffs by ear," says pianist McCoy Tyner. "Notation came later." Riffs also formed the basis of many great solos and, while used more sparingly by bop and post-bop stylists, remain one of the jazz vocabulary's most venerable devices that warrants detailed study since it provides a fundamental starting point for so many aspects of improvisation.

Frequently the terms riff and lick are used interchangeably, but they are distinctly different. A riff is a repeated idea—a kind of ostinato that can have a 1-, 2- or, 4-bar structure—whereas a lick is a memorized melodic fragment, phrase, or cliché that is not designed to be repeated. Many jazz tunes are based on riffs—especially blues. Although the riff is most often considered to be a melodic component of improvisation and composition, aspects can be effectively applied to comping and teach a great deal about phrasing, form, and structure.

Comping riffs differ from melodic riffs in several respects, but they also have a great deal in common. In a blues context, the comping riff can be a 1-, 2-, or 4-bar rhythmic idea, although 4-bar figures can take several forms and bring greater variety to the overall 12-bar structure. Since many riffs are based on rhythmic figures that may not have enough rhythmic elements to accommodate all possible chord substitutions, in some cases you may have to reduce the number of chords in a progression to its simplest form. By the same token, you should feel under no obligation to include every possible chord change in the first place—frequently a simple idea is the most effective. Furthermore, even when you are presented with the opportunity to frequently change chords, you simply may not wish to do so because it doesn't fit into your conception at the moment.

Once you develop a feel for riff comping in all of its forms, you'll be able to not only spontaneously play chorus after chorus, but also tell in advance whether or not a figure is going to work. There are seemingly endless possibilities, and many of these ideas can be applied to forms other than 12-bar blues, including 16- and 32-measure tunes. Now let's, in turn, take a look at 1-, 2-, and 4-bar figures, and then see how they can be combined with wide variety of chord voicings.

Riff Structure

1-Bar Riffs

Due to their repetitive nature, 1-bar patterns can be highly effective—both as accompaniments to heads and in building tension behind a soloist. Their downside, however, is that they can quickly become boring if overused.

To start let's take a look at perhaps the most common 1-bar rhythmic idea, the "Charleston" figure, which traditionally features an eighth-note value located on the first beat of the measure and an off-beat eighth on the "and" of two. The following example shows the Charleston figure, as well as three related variations that use the same number of elements as the original. (Adding more elements leads to numerous other possibilities; for instance, the first eighth could be divided into two sixteenth-note values.) At first their differences may seem subtle; however, when put to use they can individually yield unique results. Thinking in terms of rhythmic relatives can be a very powerful tool, so be sure to add it to your musical vocabulary.

Here are four more figures. Keeping accuracy and swing your utmost priorities, be able to count them out, tap or clap them, and imagine them in your mind's eye. In other words, become so familiar with them that you can count them in your sleep. Work out others on your own by first applying the concept of rhythmic relatives, and then move on to entirely new figures. Even if you limit yourself to rest and note values no smaller than an eighth in duration, there are many possibilities. While these work well as isolated figures, they can also serve as building blocks for 2- and 4-bar patterns.

2-Bar Riffs

These patterns have similar tension-building capabilities as 1-bar patterns, except that they are twice as long and therefore usually proportionally less prone to becoming monotonous. They can be made up of two 1-bar statements, as this, which uses the Charleston figure and a rhythmic relative—

—or be tied together to form a single idea, like this, where the second measure is anticipated by a half-beat:

Repeat each two-bar idea six times to complete the 12-bar framework.

4-Bar Riffs

These constitute not only the only the most complex riffs, but also afford variation beyond shorter figures because they raise the possibility of rhythmically imitating the AAB form of blues tunes. Let's look at the ways in which 4-bar riffs can be developed; each will be illustrated with one music example.

In this first phrase, a simple 1-bar figure is repeated three times; the 4-bar riff is then completed with a period, or finalizing statement:

The basis of the next possibility is a 2-bar idea seen earlier, but with a period that completes the 4-bar idea):

So far, you've seen varying degrees of internal repetition; however, it's also common for there to be no recurrence of figures over the course of the four measures. This pattern can be thought to be made up of a series of 1-bar ideas:

Regardless of whether a 4-bar pattern contains internal repetition, it can be played three times to complete the 12-bar cycle. However, the 4-bar riff also raises a couple of other possibilities. In one, you begin the third repetition like the previous two, except that you add a new period.

The other possibility follows the typical AAB blues phrase structure by repeating the first four measures twice, and then completing the form with four measures of entirely new material in a kind of call and response format. The following verse illustrates:

My boss mistreats me, and my ex says she's gonna sue
My boss mistreats me, and my ex says she's gonna sue
Gonna play my guitar 'till I just ain't got the blues

Here's a 4-bar riff played twice and followed by a finalizing 4-bar idea:

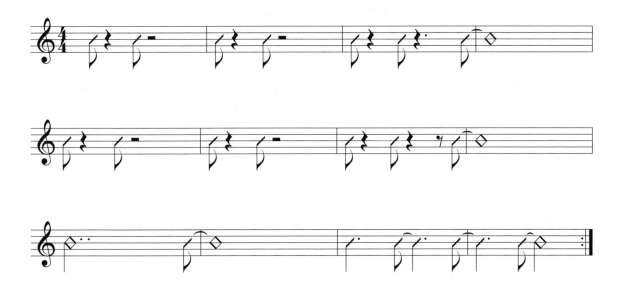

A tune's mood, tempo, and time signature may call for more active patterns (for instance, a slow blues raises the possibility of including triplet- and/or sixteenth-based figures). Regardless, riff comping will dramatically expand your ability to comp chorus after chorus, as well as give you a deeper feel for the blues. Incidentally, even when you use repetitive 1- and 2-bar figures, feel free to add a new idea in the last four measures, or a finalizing idea in bars 11 and 12, the turnaround area. Now let's see how riff comping can be combined with actual chords.

Chord Riffs—Starting Simple

The following examples illustrate how only a few chords can be applied to riff figures, creating extremely effective accompaniments. Since the guitar can accommodate an overwhelming number of voicings and chord types, no single volume could adequately cover every possibility. Nevertheless, many are featured on the pages to come.

1-Bar Riffs

B♭ Blues. This first example features two 12-bar choruses that strictly employ the Charleston figure and use common "jazz chords" voiced on the first four strings. The first chorus uses only one chord per change. Bars 11 and 12 use a I7-V7 rather than the common I7-VI7-IIm7-V7 pattern. Starting at measure 13, however, a few additional chords take advantage of the figure's rhythmic opportunities to lessen the repetition and sketch out the voice-leading a bit more completely. Bar 16 uses B♭7♯5♯9 (the same as E13, a half-step approach to E♭7). Since the measure has two different rhythmic elements (two eighth notes), two different chords could have been used, or B♭7♯5♯9 could have been postponed until the "and" of beat two. In bar 18, Edim7 is played on the second eighth, although it could have been placed on the first beat. Bars 19 and 20 descend chromatically to VI7; each chord retains B♭ in its uppermost voice. Measure 22's F11 is synonymous with Cm9. In the final two bars, observe that G7♯5♯9 is the same as D♭13, while F7♯5♯9 is the same as B13 (both are ♭5 substitutes). By the way, it's common to vary the chords from chorus to chorus; more on this in upcoming sections.

"Outside Groove"

TRACK 10

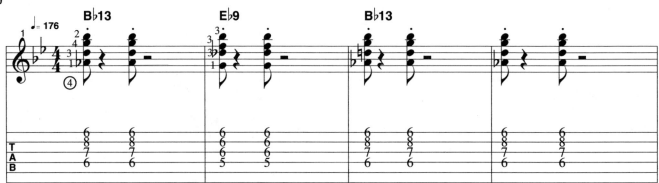

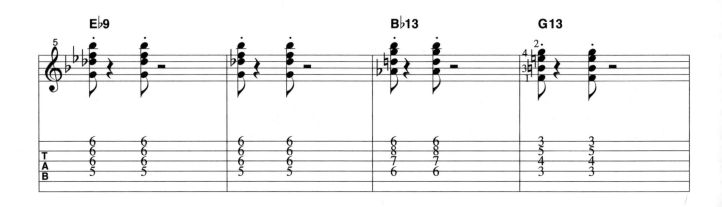

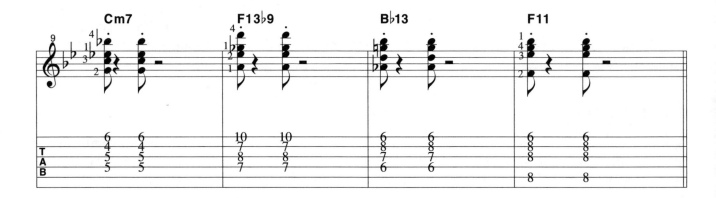

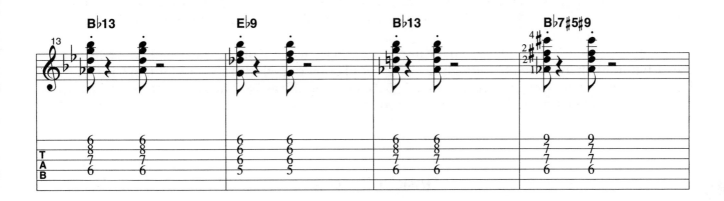

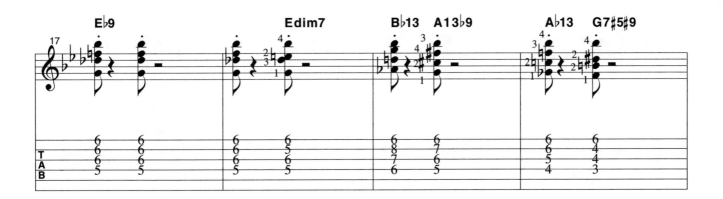

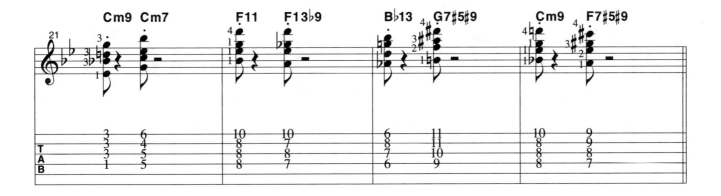

As you can see, very few chords can be extremely effective when used in the right rhythmic context. Although jazz guitarists are often admired for the many chords they play, the most important aspect is always the groove. Dozens of ultra-hip chord voicings are meaningless if they are not applied in a musically vital way. Rhythm, groove, and swing should always be the main objective. If elaborate voice-leading can then enhance the musicality of a tune, fine, but it should always play a secondary role to mood and feel.

Although no guitar book could comprehensively address every aspect of harmony as it applies to jazz guitar, a number of helpful concepts are featured in the pages ahead, including those covering block chords and voice-leading.

F Blues. Here's another very simple but effective 1-bar riff; however, now the chords are voiced on the middle four strings (make a point of knowing how identical voicings appear on different string sets; for instance, the voicing of the first chord here, F13, is identical to that of the first chord, B♭13, in the previous example).

A common tone, F, is maintained in the upper voice of each chord until measure 10, which leads to the turnaround. In measures 10 through 12, a ♯5♯9 chord is alternated with a 13th chord. In bar 11, D7♯5♯9 can also be interpreted as A♭13, while C7♯5♯9 can be viewed as G♭13, which means that the turn-around also functions as a I7-♭III7-II7-♭II7, a chromatic alternative to the usual I7-VI7-IIm7 (or II7)-V7.

"Inside Groove"

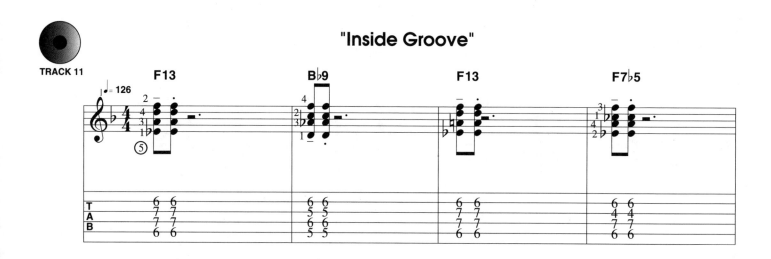

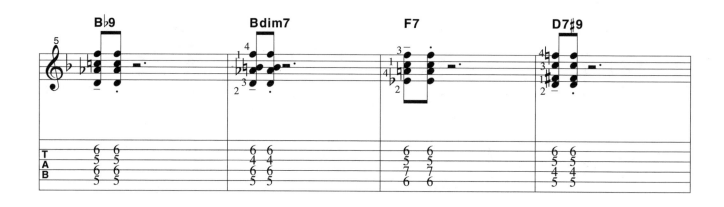

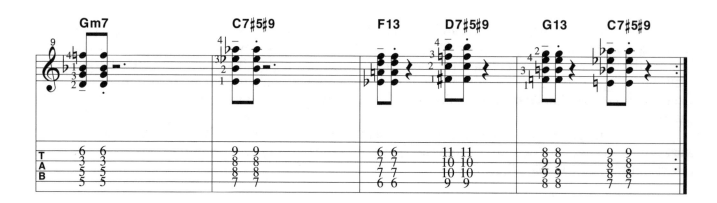

C Blues. This next example of the 1-bar riff, in the spirit of Kenny Burrell, features a funky Charleston-based groove and bluesy chords in the key of C. Observe that a common tone (here, D#/Eb) is featured in the uppermost voice until measure 9, giving the entire accompaniment a funky feel. Also notice the use of #IVdim7 on the "and" of beat two in measure 6, and G11 in bar 12, the only measure to deviate from the Charleston rhythmic pattern. Since the feel is so strong and funky, you could add a bass player and a drummer and this could practically pass for a complete tune.

TRACK 12

"K's Funky Groove"

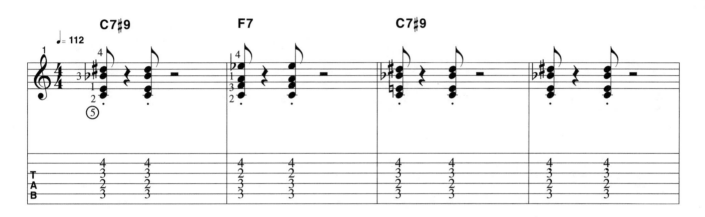

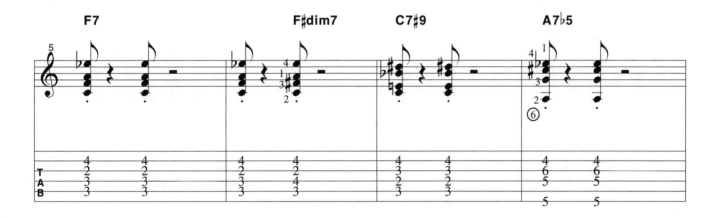

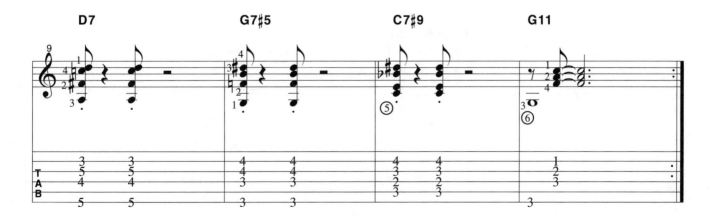

2-Bar Riffs

F Blues. While 1-bar riffs are extremely effective when used in the appropriate context, they can become boring if over-applied or misused. In contrast, 2-bar patterns offer relief from monotony and provide additional rhythmic possibilities.

The following example features a 2-bar riff in the key of F. Notice that the riff is maintained until the turnaround. The first string carries the voice-leading, which forms a simple melody. Again, the chords are common, and the turnaround features a basic I7-V7:

TRACK 13

"Every Other Bar Blues"

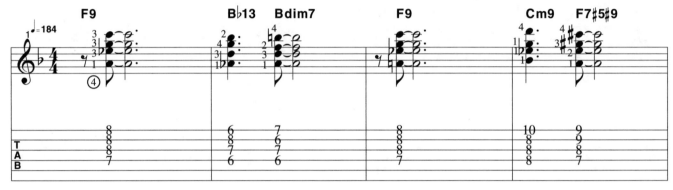

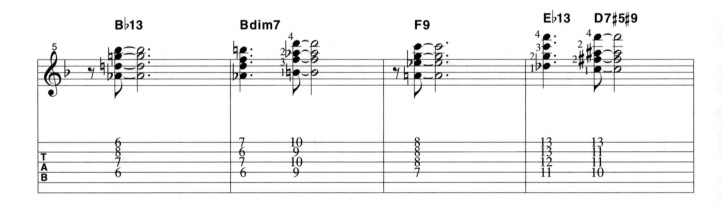

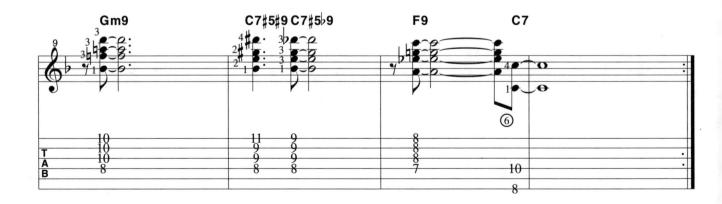

Bb Blues. This next 24-bar example features another 2-bar pattern. The first chorus is sparse and funky. The harmony is stripped down to only a double-stop—the 3rd and ♭7th of the chord at hand. The figure is maintained until measure 9, the beginning of the period, or closing statement. While the same overall idea continues in the second chorus, a secondary riff that employs three-note structures is added, which increases the activity.

Here, bar 14 moves to the subdominant (E♭7) as usual, but the "tune" (hypothetically) could just as easily remain on I7 until measure 17, which would actually be appropriate for the idea's overall funky feel. Playing a supporting role on the guitar often implies using relatively complete structures with three or more notes; however, frequently you only need to suggest the harmony. In this case, that is accomplished with only two critical notes.

"Double-Stop Soul"

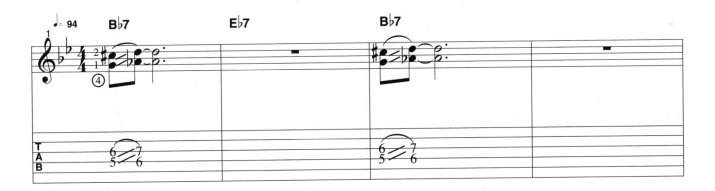

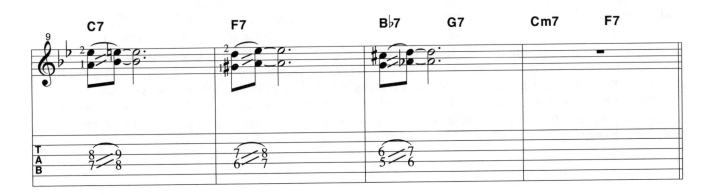

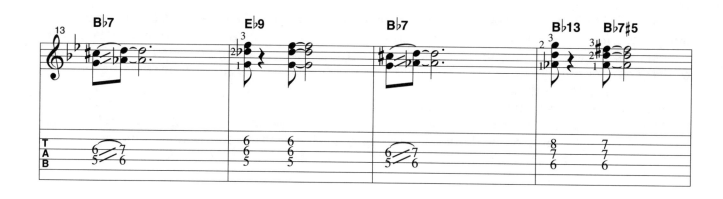

Notice that the secondary, or answering riff of the preceding example's second chorus is based on the Charleston rhythm. In addition to featuring a contrasting rhythmic figure, it introduces a voice-leading element that often runs counter to the riff itself. For example, in measure 15, the riff moves from C♯ to D, while the following "answer" in bar 16 counters by moving from G down to F♯. In addition to being a useful strategy that can be applied to arranging in general (including writing big-band charts), thinking in terms of counter or secondary riffs can be highly effective—not only when the guitar is the only harmonic instrument, but also in terms of supplying fills in an ensemble context.

Changing the rhythm of measure 16 would, of course, transform what was a 2-bar riff into a 4-bar riff, opening up the rhythmic possibilities even further. Before we consider that in more detail, look at this next 2-bar riff.

C Blues. This example is a continuation and elaboration of "Kenny's Funky Groove" on page 39 and, among other things, points out that you don't need to adhere to a single riff when you comp with a rhythm section. For this chorus, the Charleston figure is displaced by one beat in the first measure (so that it begins on the second beat), while the second bar uses the Charleston rhythm with an added quarter-note on beat four. Together, they form a 2-bar syncopated riff that suggests a Latin clave figure—in a blues context, no less! The 2-bar idea is continued until measure 9, which introduces a close, or finalizing idea. Try playing the two versions of "K's Funky Groove" one after another—it presents quite a challenge. Practice until you can make a seamless transition from the first to the second chorus, while accurately playing the rhythms.

TRACK 14

"K's Funky Groove 2"

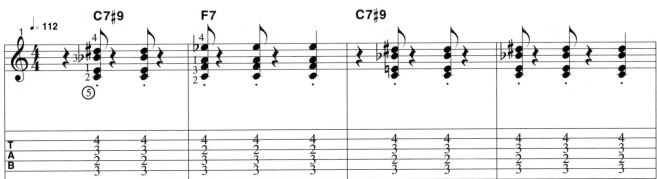

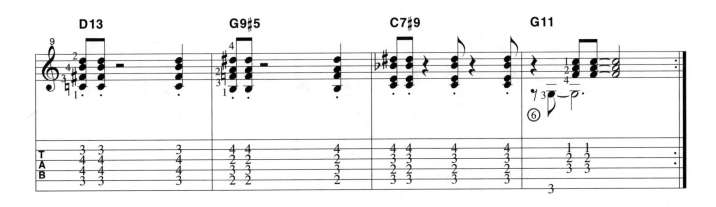

4-Bar Riffs

B♭ Blues. This first illustration of a 4-bar riff is based on a figure favored by George Barnes. Although it can be used as an accompaniment, its active rhythms and aggressive quality also enable it to function as a shout chorus. (The diagonal lines indicate a "fall," which is notated a bit differently than it would be in a typical arranger's score for jazz band; here the fall should last approximately two beats.) Instead of repeating the same 4-bar phrase three times, the structure closely adheres to the 12-bar blues song form. The first two 4-bar phrases each close a bit differently, while, measure 9 again introduces a 4-bar period. The tempo is relatively bright, and the chord voicings are primarily played on the first four strings.

TRACK 15

"Four By George"

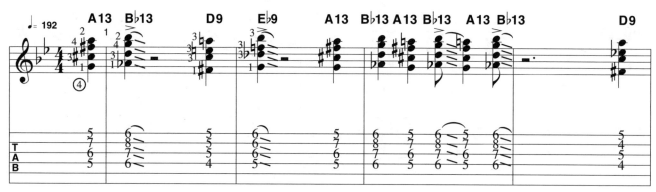

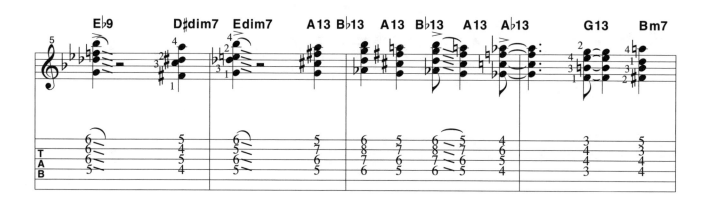

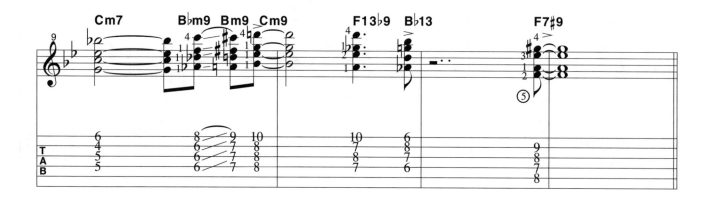

Eb **Blues.** "One For Barney" was inspired by the great Barney Kessel, who melded swing's extensive use of riffs and a rollicking sense of time with the sophisticated harmonies of bebop. Here, notice the open voicings and that the second string carries the upper note of the chord. In contrast to the common tone in the upper voice, the lowest is constantly moving throughout the 12-bars. (Keep in mind that it is also possible to create a moving inner line, even when maintaining an upper common tone.) Like the preceding example, this one also follows the blues song structure.

The bebop element is reflected by the opening measure, which begins with Eb11 (it could just as easily been called Bbm11, making the opening sequence a IIm7-V7 of IV7, a relatively common bebop practice). The second four bars close a bit differently and move chromatically downward to VI7 (C7#9).

The last four measures constitute a period. In measure 9, Gm7#5 is purely a "passing" chord that connects root-position Fm7 to first-inversion Fm7.

"One For Barney"

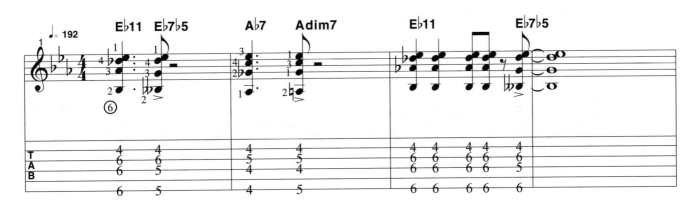

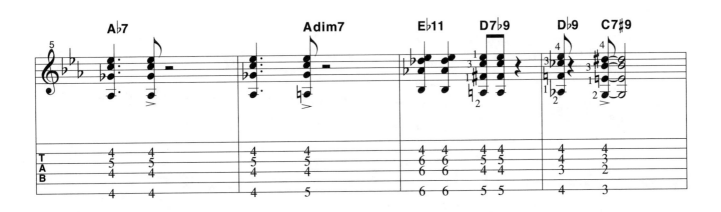

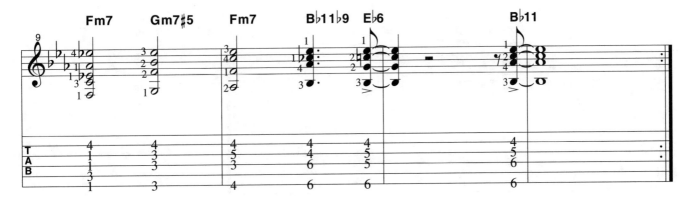

G Blues. While this last chorus is more of a head than an accompaniment and doesn't strictly adhere to the characteristics of the 4-bar riff that have been discussed, it's included because of its hip moves. Again the blues song structure is followed.

The riff itself uses a funky single-note line. Remember that you could go to IV7 in bar 2 by playing what's in bar 5, including its pickup and the three notes that lead back to I7. Notice the C#dim7 chord that punctuates the riff in measure 6, and how VI7 (E7#9) is approached in bar 8. Measure 9 features a walking line played in octaves. Bar 10 is based solely on the G blues scale, while 11 features a common octave-based turnaround.

"Turkey Bacon"

Bebop—Linear Comping

While the line between swing and bebop is often fine, the latter is generally more linear—not only melodically, but also rhythmically. This is in large part due to bebop's abundance of chord changes, which precludes the extensive use of riff figures common to swing and results in increased rhythmic freedom. Linearity and more chords also increases the possibilities in terms of voice-leading.

Again, the guitar is capable of accommodating a vast number of voice-leading possibilities—from the formal, harmony-text variety that encompasses aspects like contrary motion and often requires fingerstyle technique, to modal and chromatic movement that is more associated with jazz. Since including an example of each type would have prevented this book from dealing in depth with any one of them, this section is primarily limited to the use of block chords. Still, it features not only a broad array of blues treatments, but also a wide variety of chords, hip connections, and other concepts.

Block Chords

The chords already used in this chapter fall under this heading and are fixed fingerings, formations, or shapes that are usually limited to four notes. Since they are generally easy to finger, they can be spontaneously threaded together—not only stating a tune's harmonic structure, but also so that their uppermost note forms a line that complements the music overall and even directly reacts with the soloist in a musical way.

Remember that block chords are voice-led in much the same way as "fat chords," except that they function in a higher register and, consequently, their uppermost voice is usually carried by either the first or second string, instead of the third. In contrast to three-note chords, though, since they usually accommodate extensions or alterations (often in the top voice) and are played in a relatively rhythmically free manner, they have a great deal more melodic flexibility and potential. While connections from the upper voice of one chord to that of the next can be smooth and closely related (maintaining a common tone, or moving either chromatically or by step), wide intervals can also be incorporated. Moreover, a chord phrase can end at any number of points, enabling you to creatively begin a new idea in a lower register and then work your way up in pitch or move up and then work down. In short, they afford a great deal of leeway for expression and invention.

Fingerboard Organization—Chord Scales

Although chords can be learned individually in isolation, they can also frequently be systematized in ways that makes them not only easier to learn, but also easier to use. One method involves thinking in terms of chord scales. The following example features direct harmonization of the G Mixolydian mode, which ascends on the first string. ("Direct" refers to the fact that a G dominant chord is used to support, or harmonize, each note of the mode.) For each note, this example offers only one supporting chord. Furthermore, for the sake of simplicity, no alterations are employed. Remember, there are many possibilities; find other supporting chords on your own (you needn't restrict yourself to the first four strings). Also observe that you can ascend one way and descend another. (Other organizational ideas are discussed on page 64.)

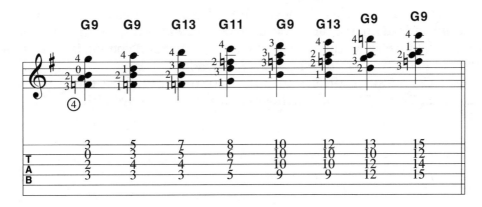

The next chord scale is a direct harmonization of every note of the chromatic scale, except for the ♮7th degree, which is omitted due to the focus on dominant chords. Notice the use of of altered chords. Again, there are many possibilities for harmonizing each tone.

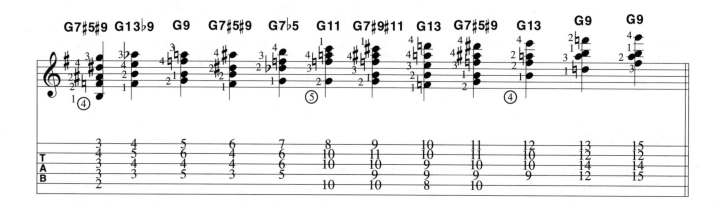

Transpose the preceding chord scales to all keys. Of course, the more chords you know, the more options are at your disposal for threading them together. While the voice-leading possibilities with block chords are somewhat limited, they still enable you to often integrate moving lines (internal or external), as well as employ common tones. In the examples to come, instances of these devices will be noted as they occur.

Basic Voice-Leading

B♭ Blues. While many of the chords of the next two examples were introduced earlier, here they are used in a freer rhythmic context.

Ideas for this first two-chorus example in B♭ grew out of jamming with the late great Lenny Breau one afternoon, as he played one subtle blues variation after another. Rhythmically, the approach is linear overall, and the chords—including several altered structures—closely follow the jazz version of the standard 12-bar blues progression.

The pickup anticipates measure 1's I7 chord; E13 can be thought of either as a half-step approach to bar 2's IV7 (E♭9, which anticipates the second measure by an eighth value) or as B♭7♯5♯9, a direct substitute for I7. In bar 2, Edim7 connects IV7 to I7.

Measure 3 features a common, effective device used by Barney Kessel and many others—a half-step movement away from and back to the same chord. Here the initial motion is upward from B♭13 to B13, but the idea works equally well if you move down to A13. Another anticipation is used at the end of bar 4, while measure 6 again features a diminished 7th connection to I7.

Bars 8 and 9 use a Charleston relative. Note the altered structure in measures 8, 9, and 10. Bars 11 and 12 go from B♭13 to G7♯9 to C7♯5♯9, which moves down chromatically to F13.

The second chorus, beginning at measure 13, has a less active rhythmic scheme that uses longer values. Bar 15 features a different rhythmic twist on the half-step movement away from and back to the same chord that was just discussed.

At the end of measure 19, VI7 is anticipated by an eighth value. Notice the altered chord (G7♯5♯9) used for VI7. Like the preceding chorus, this structure is moved down one half-step for II7 (C13), and then taken down one half-step more to realize V7 (F7♯5♯9). This same type of chromatic device is again applied to the turnaround.

Another aspect of this example—and the ones to come—bears mentioning: the fact that it doesn't strictly follow the same chord changes from chorus to chorus. While here the deviation is slight, in other cases it may be more striking. Regardless, let your ears, which should always be open to your surroundings, guide you. The degree to which you can embellish a basic chord progression depends on a variety of factors, including the instrumentation of the ensemble you happen to be playing with and how familiar the members are with each other. If the guitar is the only chordal instrument, then the opportunities for varying a progression are broad. Even when the bass player or soloist momentarily goes in a different direction, odds are that it will work with what you are doing—often merely due to the fact that everything is going by so fast that it's difficult to notice the resulting incongruities. Ultimately, though, knowledgeable musicians listen carefully so they can complement and change direction at a moment's notice.

"Jammin' With Lenny"

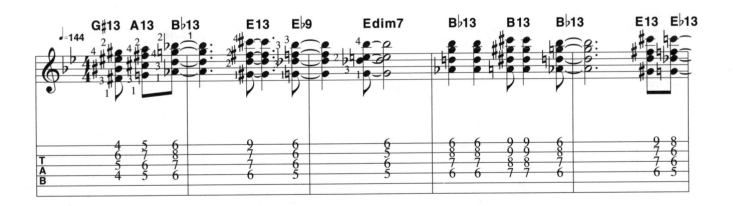

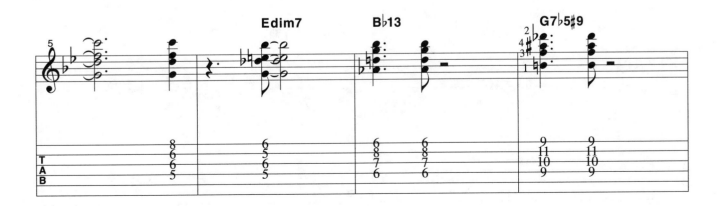

All Blues

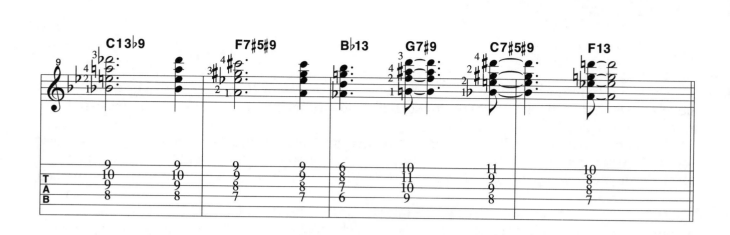

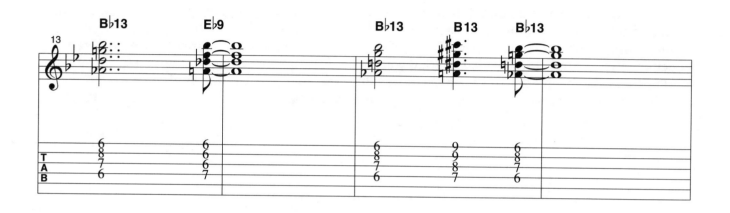

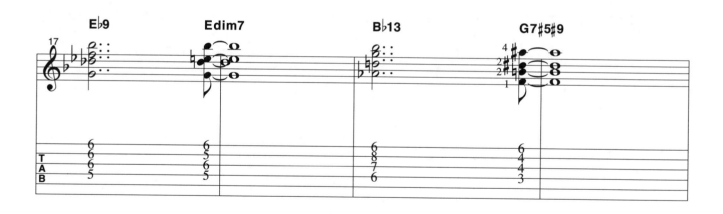

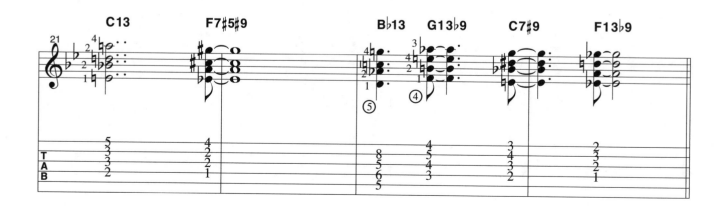

F Blues. The next two choruses fairly closely adhere to the standard blues progression. Overall, the rhythms are spacious and again linear.

The pickup moves chromatically to I7 (F9), and A13 on the fourth beat of bar 1 approaches IV7 from a half-step below. In measure 6, Bdim7 connects IV7 (B♭13) to I7 (F9), while bar 9 features a closely voiced Gm9 (IIm7), which resolves nicely to C7♭9♯11 (V7) in measure 10.

The ascending motion in the first measure of the second chorus (bar 13) is assisted by F♯dim7, a passing chord that connects I7 to IV7. In bar 16, A13 approaches IV7 (B♭13) from a half-step below. Finally, measure 20 features a common tone (F) as VI7 (D7♯5♯9) is approached from a half-step above.

TRACK 17

"Bebop Groove"

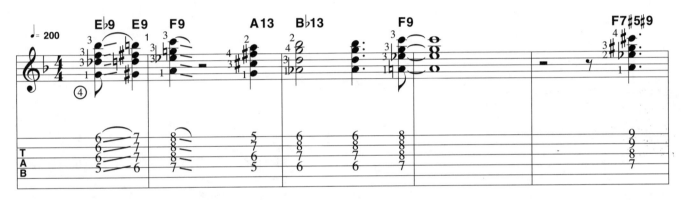

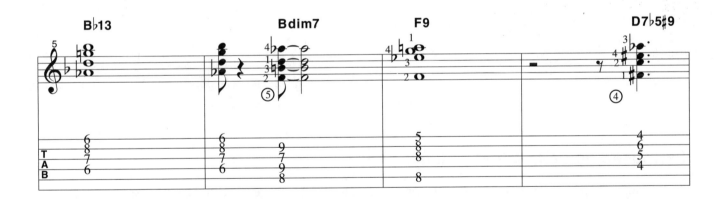

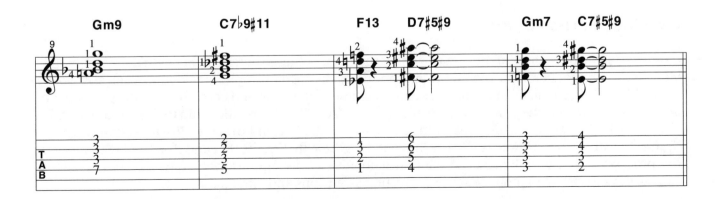

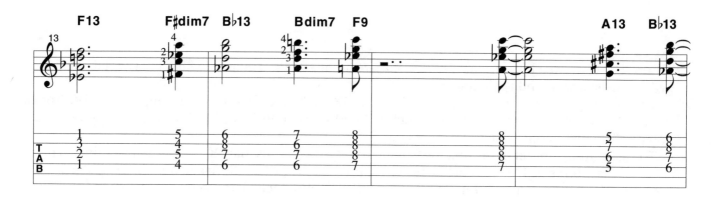

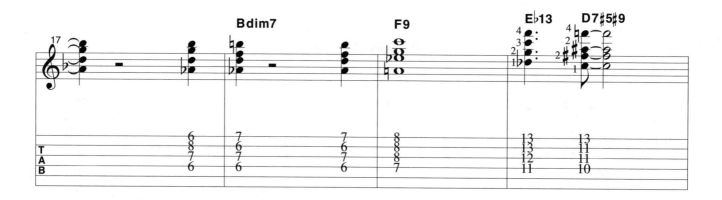

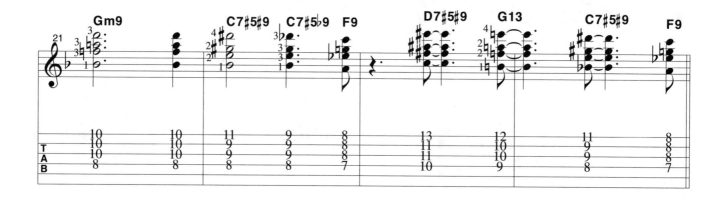

Increased Voice-Leading Activity

In the next examples, the voice-leading is more calculated. The net result is longer phrases and smoother upper-voice motion.

The Blues Scale Factor

C Blues. Voicing the chords of the jazz version of the 12-bar blues progression beneath the notes of the blues scale can produce some incredibly hip sounds, as this next example, in C, demonstrates. As you apply this idea, keep the relationship between each note of the scale and each chord in the progression in mind. For instance, the C blues scale reads C, Eb, F, F#/Gb, G, Bb. In relationship to C7, C is the root, Eb is the #9th, F is the 11th, F# is the b5th (or raised 11th), G is the 5th, and Bb is the b7th. In relationship to F7, C is the 5th, Eb is the lowered 7th, F is the root, F# is the b9th, G is the 9th, and Bb is the 11th. Continue this process on your own. While every chord will not necessarily support every note, the ones that do can be very effective and produce some interesting extensions and alterations.

Analyze the following example, especially noting the half-step approaches and the turnaround. While this example exclusively uses the notes of the blues scale in the upper voice of the chords, the idea can be expanded to include other notes and concepts—as seen in not only some of the examples you've already encountered, but also some of the ones to come.

"Uptown Funk"

B♭ Blues. In the first three measures of "Twelfth Inning Stretch," notice how the high D note descends to F on the second string. In measure 3, a chromatic phrase that begins on the "and" of beat three leads to bar 4's Fm7, a common substitute for I7. However, instead of forming a IIm7-V7 of E♭9, it moves down chromatically to E13, which in turn resolves to E♭9. (In other words, instead of preceding E♭9 with a temporary IIm7-V7, IIm7-♭II7 is used.)

A nice chord cliché begins on the "and" of bar 5's fourth beat and continues into measure 7. While the chords can be analyzed in more than one way, they are more a product of voicing the melodic line

C-A-F. The phrase in measures 7 and 8 is equally nice, where inversions of B♭9 and B♭13 lead up to G7♯5♭9 (enharmonic to D♭9).

After bar 9's Cm7 voicings, there are a couple of common but nice sequences. One comes in measure 10 where F11, which could also be thought of as Cm11, leads to F13♭9. While here the sequence is applied to a dominant context, it could also serve as a IIm7-V7, where each chord is played for two beats. Another nice IIm7-V7 is used in measure 12 (transfer the voicings to strings two through five, and you're liable to discover its source).

Bars 13 through 15 feature a common sequence (notice the B♭ common tone). Measure 16 again uses the IIm7-V7 of E♭ idea found in the preceding chorus. Instead of moving back to I7 by means of ♯IVdim7, however, a dim7 passing chord voice-leads to IVm7-♭VII7—the common "back door" approach to I7. From the last part of bar 20 to the end, a series of interesting "inside" chords—voiced on strings two through five—complete the comping pattern. Analyze this section carefully on your own; these versatile chords have many uses.

Again, use caution when you play though different changes from chorus to chorus.

"Twelfth Inning Stretch"

TRACK 19

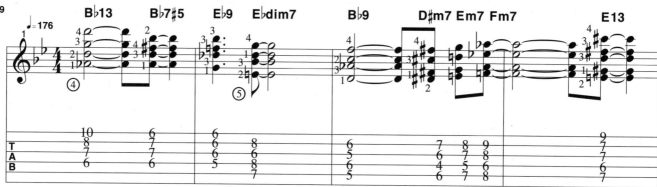

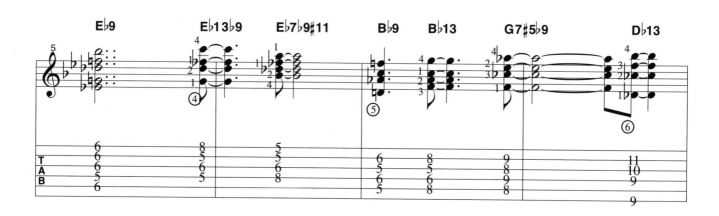

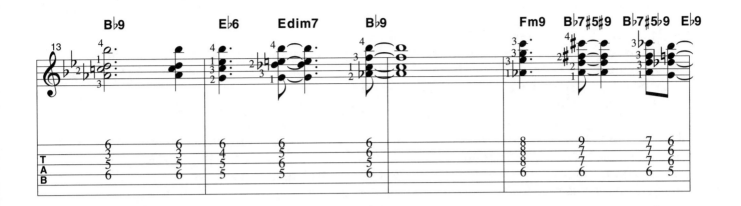

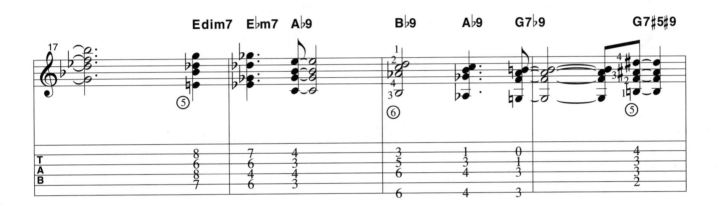

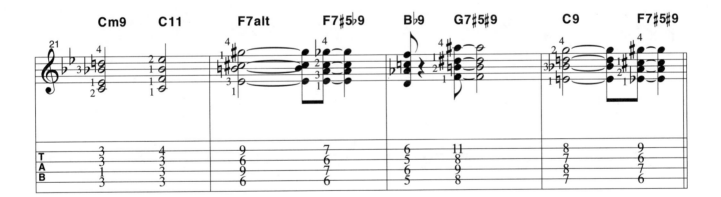

F Blues. Here, voice-leading is emphasized yet again. In the first three measures, notice the long phrase that starts on high D and moves down to second string A.

Bar 4 features a common bop resolution—a IIm7-V7 that's a half-step above the target chord (in this case, Bb9). Remember that you can also think of this as a IIm7-V7 based on the b5 substitute of F7, which is the V7 of Bb (the b5 sub of F7 is B7).

The chords in measures 5 and 6 are a common guitar move, as are the ones in bars 9 and 10 and 11 and 12 (measure 12's C7b9#11 is typical of voicings played by Tal Farlow that require the thumb for a sixth- or fifth-string bass note).

The second chorus uses a sequence seen before: I7-IV7-#IVdim7-I7. In measure 16, inside chords are used to realize a nice IIm7-V7 of B♭9.

Bar 18 is also interesting and common. While it begins to suggest a "back door" approach to I7, instead it moves down by half-steps (IVm7-♭VII7-IIIm7-VI7-♭IIIm7-VI7) until measure 21's Gm9 (IIm7) is reached. Again, sparingly use this kind of variation.

The last four measures feature more close voicings. At the end of measure 21, Am9 makes a nice passing chord leading to C11. In bar 23, D7alt (so named due to the large number of alterations) could also be thought of as F7♯9. Finally, measure 24 features another common and effective guitar move. Although it's sometimes appropriate to limit yourself to certain types of voicings and repetitive riff-based rhythmic figures, it's usually best to remain flexible and open to a wide variety of devices, as these choruses illustrate. In the long run, flexibility keeps you listening intently so you can spontaneously react and respond to the music around you, possibly imitating ideas at one moment, filling voids the next, and extending phrases at another. As always, the more approaches, chords, fingerboard command, rhythms, and general experience you have at your disposal, the more equipped you'll be to make a choice that is musical.

"Thinkin' Tal"

TRACK 20

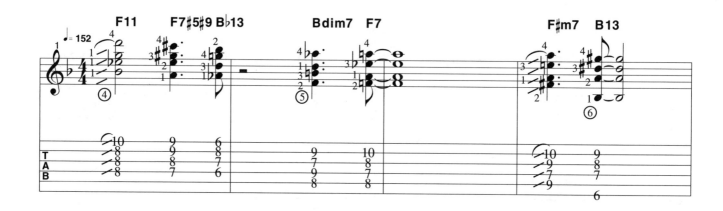

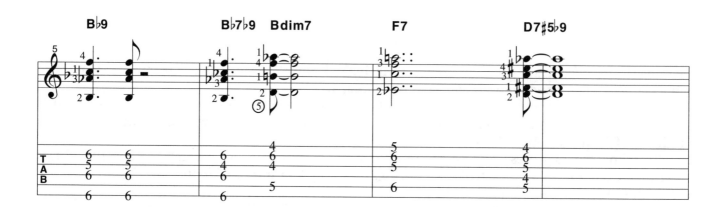

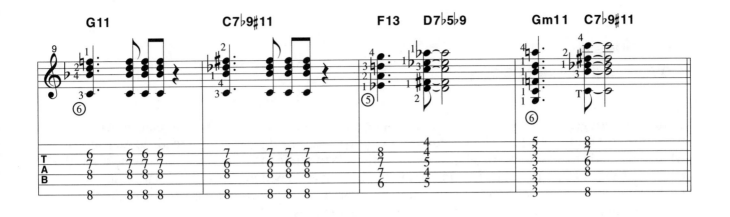

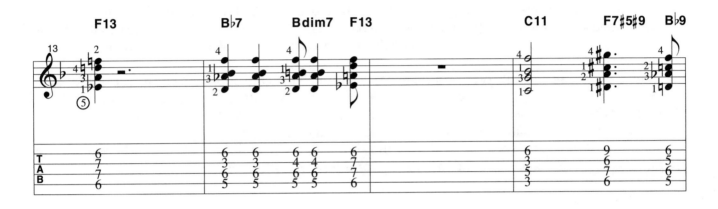

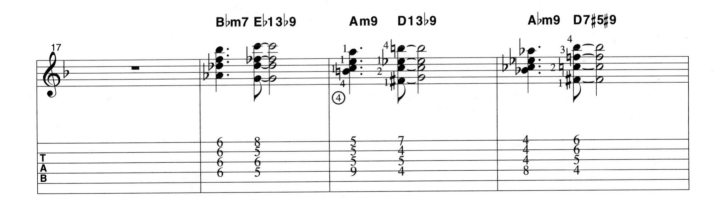

Slow Blues &
Advanced Voice Leading

G Blues. Although Joe Pass and Joe Diorio are especially great at voice-leading that features a chord per beat, this next example is more for demonstration purposes than it represents a realistic example of what you can do in a practical playing situation. Still, it is possible to voice-lead this extensively in the context of a slow blues (note the tempo marking). The degree to which you adhere to the chord-per-beat format is, of course, entirely up to you and may vary from portions of a tune to the entire thing. Here, a wide variety of voicings, inversions, and chord qualities are employed. As you work your way through the example, pay particular attention to line formed by the upper voice of each chord.

The first chorus is linear in quality. On the fourth beat of bar 1, Db13 resolves to C13 from a half-step above. In measure 2, #IVdim7 (C#dim7) resolves to bar 3's Vm7 (here, Dm9) instead of the usual I7 in second-inversion. Remember: A Vm7-I7-IV7 is equivalent to a IIm7-V7 of IV7, where IV7 is treated as a temporary I7 chord.

Bars 5 and 6—all basically IV7—feature two nice internal half-step approaches. The same device is used in measures 7 (which moves to IV7; here, C7#9, initially) and 8. Bar 9 uses three different qualities of Am7 chords before it moves to Eb13, which resolves down to D13 in measure 10. The turnaround (bars 11 and 12) uses a combination of lush voicings and half-step approaches.

In contrast, the upper-voice line of the second chorus is based on this four-bar riff, whose repetitive nature creates some challenges and interesting common-tone situations:

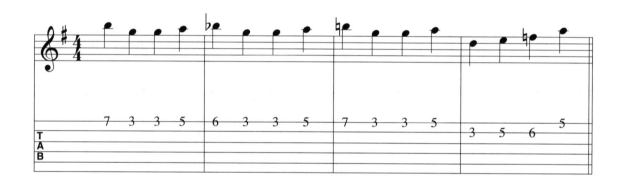

In measure 13, notice the descending internal moving line: E-D#-D. At the beginning of bar 14, Gm7 substitutes for C7. The last beat of bar 14 to the first beat of bar 15 features contrary motion: bass G moves down to F, while melodic Bb moves up to B♮. It all demonstrates that you can achieve almost any type of voice-leading with block chords. More contrary motion: this time, between measure 3's third and fourth beats (Abalt equals Ab7#5b9#9, a half-step approach to bar 16's G9).

Measures 17 and 18—all basically C7 (IV7)—include several half-step approaches, while the last two beats of bar 19 through the first two beats of measure 20 feature two consecutive IIm7-V7's that, in the key of G, translate into Vm7-I7 (Dm11-G7b5) and IVm7-bVII7 (Cm7b5-F9). Half-step approaches are used from the last beat of bar 20 to the first beat of measure 22. Finally, carefully analyze the turnaround, which moves from I7 to IV7 to IIIm7 to VI7 to IIm7 to V7 in the space of eight beats.

A slow blues can accommodate many identities: from riff treatments seen earlier in this volume to triplet feels to the elaborate voice-leading here. Let your feel and understanding—heart and soul—for the blues point the way.

"Blues For Two Joes"

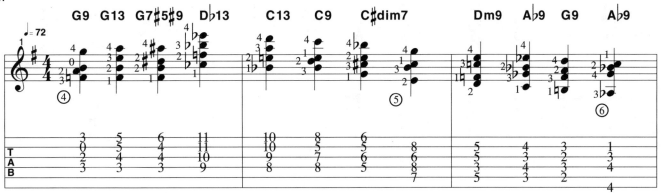

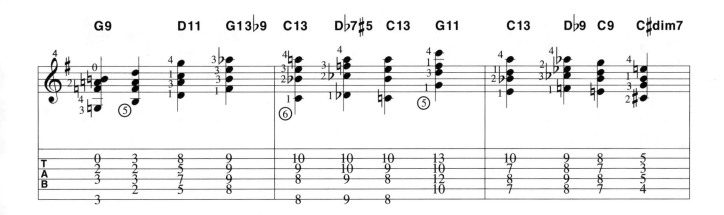

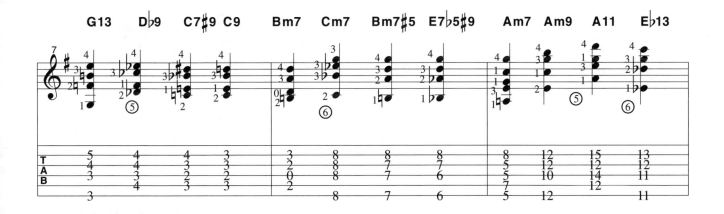

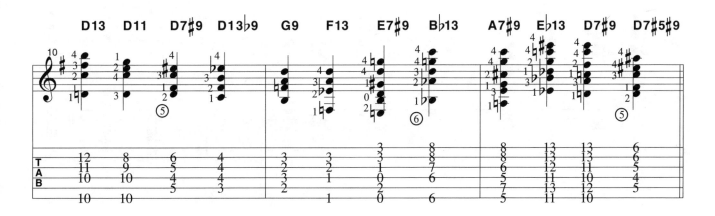

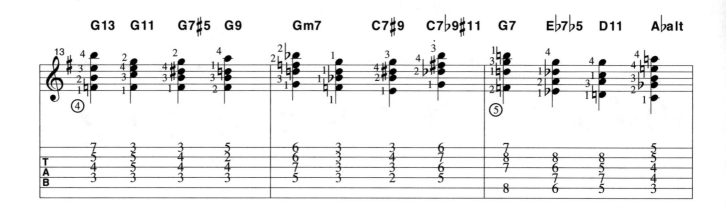

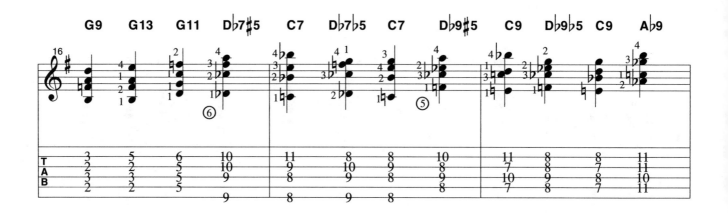

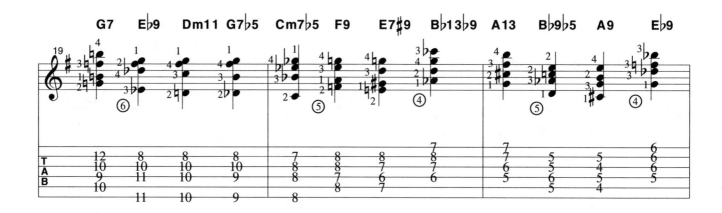

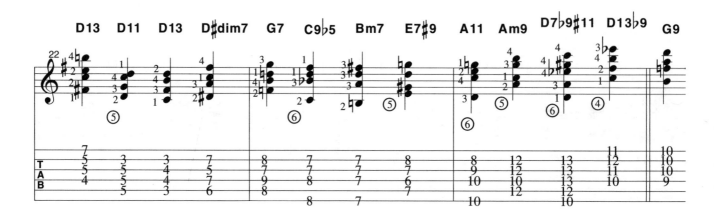

Beyond Bebop

Triads Over Bass Notes

While there are many chordal concepts beyond the bebop sphere that can be used in a blues context, space and scope limit this volume to two possibilities. The first involves structures comprising a triad plus a bass note, which can produce some intriguing results.

If this harmonic technique is unfamiliar, begin by taking a triad (either root position, first inversion, or second inversion) and placing every possible bass note beneath it. In the following example, a first-inversion B♭ triad is voiced above a chromatic bass line:

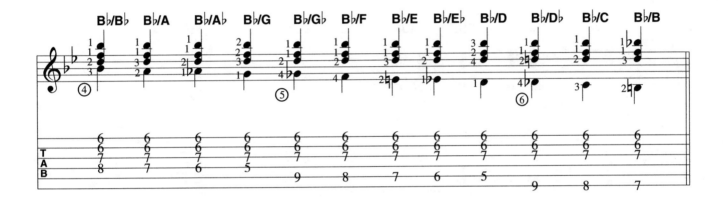

Since three of the preceding configurations are merely triads with one of the voices doubled (B♭/B♭; B♭/D; B♭/F) and one is a third-inversion 7th chord (B♭/A♭), it is the remaining structures that provide the most potential for non-standard applications. To fluently apply these, it is important to be aware of both the triad/bass note relationship and the overall composite name or names (for example, B♭/A equals B♭maj7, Gm9, E♭maj9♭5, and so on). While any triad can be voiced over any bass note, the following examples primarily use majors and minors. Since only the triad/bass note name is given, keep the standard 12-bar blues changes in mind. (Triads over bass notes are sometimes referred to as "slash chords.")

Standard Structure, New Results

B♭ Blues. The first three bars feature root-position major triads. In measure 1, E♭/F equals B♭11, while D♭/D is the same as B♭7♯9. From the last part of measure 1 to the first part of measure 2, the D♭ major triad remains stationary as the bass note changes. (D♭/E♭ equals E♭11.) Measure 2 also features C/D♭, which is the same as E♭13♭9. Measure 3 uses a second-inversion major triad to produce a structure that equals B♭7♯9. Overall, simple whole- and half-step triadic movement results in some very interesting voice-leading. Bar four retains the same bass note (D) as the preceding measure; F♯/D is the same as B♭7♯5♯9.

Conveying a distinct IV7 sound can be difficult with triads over bass notes; while bar 5's chord symbol is notated with a slash, it is really a third-inversion dominant 7th. On the "and" of the same measure, A/D♯ implies a diminished sound, functioning as ♯IVdim7.

D♭/D on the "and" of bar 6's fourth beat again functions as I7 (here, B♭7♯9). Subsequently, the structure is moved up a whole-step (E♭/E) and then a half-step (E/F), where it functions as measure 8's VI7 (here, G13♭9). Also in bar 8, A♭m/D equals G7♯5♭9. From measure 8 to measure 9, moving A♭m/D to Gm/E♭ not only results in contrary motion, but also conveys the change from VI7 to IIm7.

Finally we arrive at the turnaround. Although the letter names of the triads suggest strict ascending motion, they are voiced so that the upper note behaves more melodically. At the same time, the bass line ascends chromatically. The result features a combination of similar and contrary motion that resolves to B♭add9, which begins the hypothetical second chorus.

"Mick's Blues"

TRACK 22

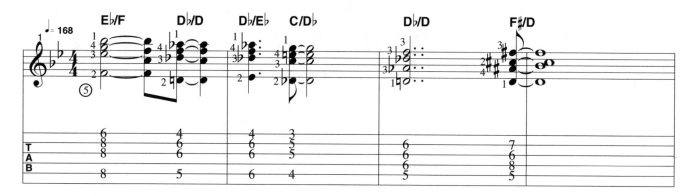

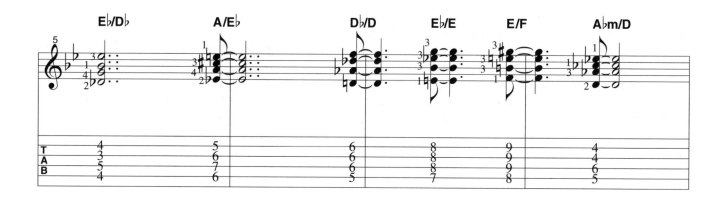

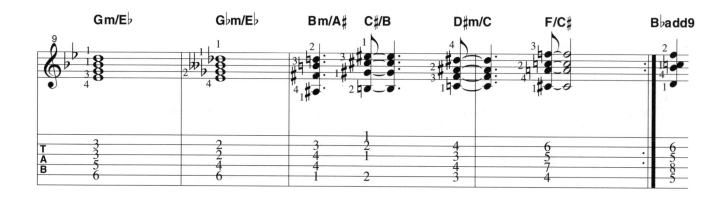

F Blues. This chorus shares many features with the preceding example. Again, keep the basic blues changes in mind as you look at the chord symbols.

In the first three measures, a root-position triad moves down chromatically. Coupled with the indicated bass notes, the symbols are equivalent to F11-F13$\flat$9-B$\flat$7$\sharp$9-B$\flat$m13$\flat$5-F11.

Again, conveying a distinct IV7 sound in a blues context can be difficult with triads over bass notes. Consequently, although the symbol in bar 5 is indicated as Fm/B$\flat$, it is really only a B$\flat$9. In measure 6, E$\flat$/D functions as B$\flat$7 and E/F functions as $\sharp$IVdim7, resolving to bar 7's F/E$\flat$, a third-inversion F7 chord.

A$\flat$/D, on the "and" of bar 7's fourth beat, equals D7$\flat$5$\flat$9 (VI7); the A$\flat$ triad resolves down a half-step to measure 9's G/D$\sharp$. The ensuing chords up to the end of measure 10 impart diminished sounds that imply G7 (II7) and then C7 (V7). Finally, observe the contrary motion In bar 11, as bass B moves to C and upper-voice C moves down to B$\flat$.

"Down Pat"

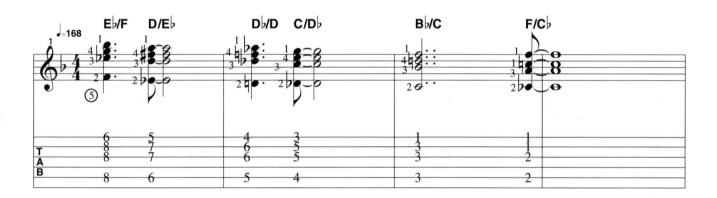

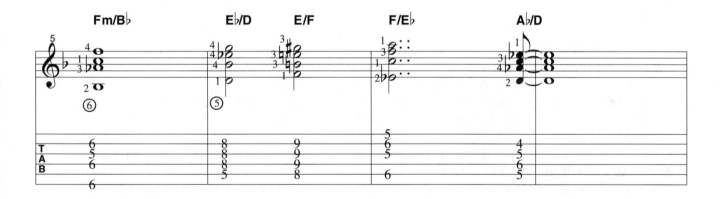

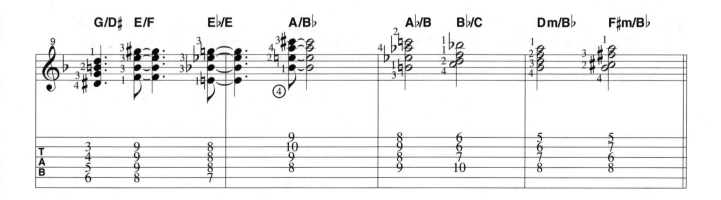

Modal Concepts

While modal tunes can accommodate any number of comping approaches—including riff figures that use few chords and linear, bebop-like rhythms that incorporate a wide array of inversions and voicings—by definition they also enable you to draw ideas from the diatonically harmonized scale of the prevailing chord at any given moment. Since most modal tunes feature very few chord changes and thereby provide an opportunity to explore possibilities that rapidly changing harmonies preclude, they usually rely upon the traditional I7-IV7-V7 progression instead of the basic sequence common to swing and bebop. In other words, a typical modal blues is the marriage of an old chord pattern and a progressive harmonic concept.

Since the prevailing tonality of I7-IV7-V7 chords is dominant, comping ideas can be drawn from the diatonically harmonized Mixolydian mode. Although any number of voicings and inversions can provide a starting point for harmonizing any given scale or mode, the following example begins with a common G13 chord (the subsequent structures are derived by moving each of G13's notes up to its next position in the mode; in effect it's as if four Mixolydian modes are being played simultaneously, each one starting at a different point):

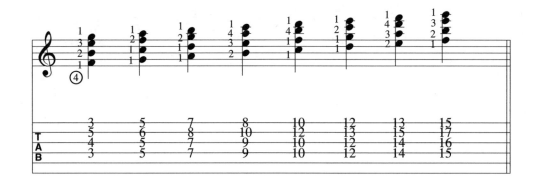

Harmonized modes, like the preceding example, can be viewed in several ways at the same time. Here are three possibilities, all of which can be useful depending on the situation:

1. In diatonically harmonized fashion, where the letter name of each successive structure advances to its next position in the alphabet, in which case the harmonies of the preceding example could be identified like so: G13, Am7♯5, Bm7♯5, Cmaj13, Dm13, Em7♯5, and Fmaj13.

2. In "direct" fashion, where each successive structure is though to be related to the "parent" (here, G13). For example, the preceding chords could be identified as G13, G11, Gadd9, G11, G11, G11, G13. (Observe that the limitations of chord symbolization results in two structures called G13 and four called G11; closely analyze chords with the same name to familiarize yourself with their subtle differences.)

3. In terms of synonymous structures. For instance, the preceding example's second harmony can be viewed as G11, Am7♯5, Dm11, and so on.

In practical terms, whenever a tune features a single chord for a relatively extended period, depending on the tempo, you can create comping phrases by threading together structures based on its harmonized mode. As you do so, keep in mind that some structures may convey a stronger sense of the chord at hand than others and that the weaker ones should generally be viewed as passing chords that connect one strong point to another.

Modal Comping

G Blues. This two-chorus example features ideas suggested by playing with Lenny Breau. The first four measures are based on I7; the first three remain within the prevailing mode, while bar four features a chromatic phrase that leads to IV7. (Notice that on the "and" of measure 4's fourth beat, the prevailing mode changes to C Mixolydian.)

When the tune moves back to I7 on the "and" of bar 6's fourth beat, two structures (G11 and G6add9) that are unrelated to the harmonized mode used for the beginning of the piece are employed. Mixing related and unrelated voicings is another common device that affords many other possibilities. Here, both structures retain the G Mixolydian tonality and feature an internal common tone (A).

Measure 8 uses a chromatic idea that resolves to V7 (D11). And in measure 10, the mode briefly switches to C Mixolydian. The final two measures avoid the swing/bebop cycle-based turnaround.

Bars 14 and 15 of the second chorus are again based on G Mixolydian, while measure 16 chromatically moves to IV7 (C13).

Bars 17 and 18 are based on the C Mixolydian mode for the most part, and resolve back to I7. Measure 19 uses an internal half-step approach (A♭9 back to G9) while bar 20 approaches D13 from a half-step above.

Again, the last two bars avoid the cycle-based turnaround.

"Trane Stop"

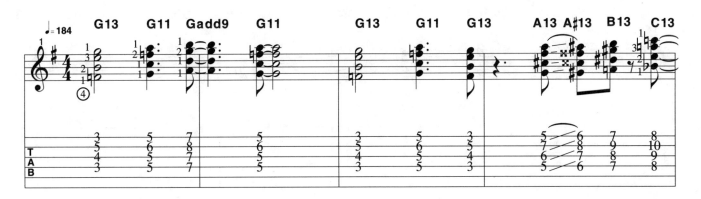

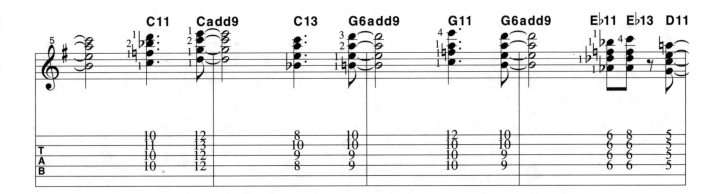

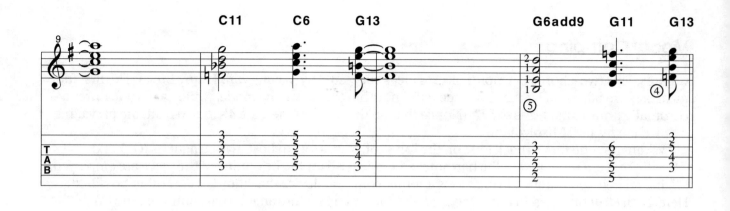

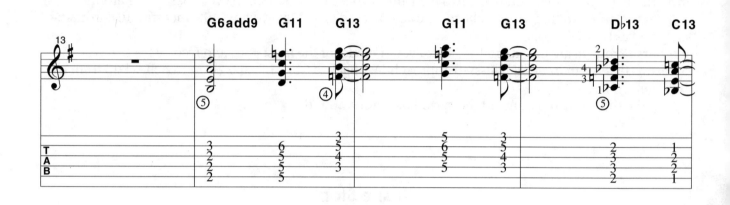

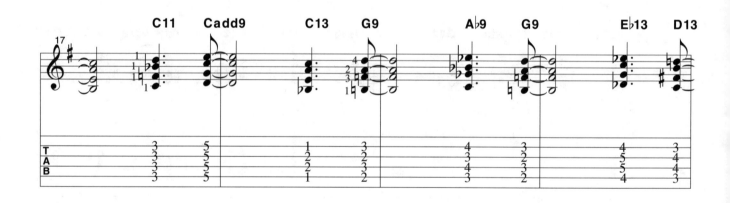

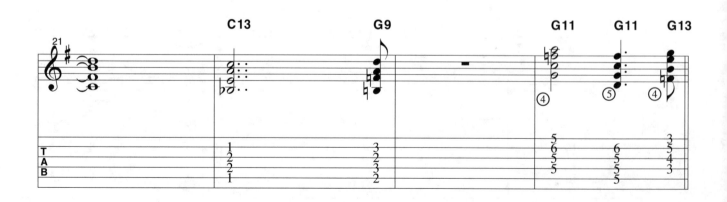

Afterthoughts

Depending on style, taste, tempo, and mood, a wide variety of approaches can be applied to any given tune. While riff ideas, linear phrases, triads over bass notes, and modal concepts have been presented in this chapter as separate entities, remember that it is possible to integrate them in a single performance. Exactly how it is done is up to your own imagination and taste.

4 YOUR FINGERS DO THE WALKING— BASS LINE/CHORD COMPING

Playing fingerstyle walking bass lines and chords at the same time is one of the hippest sounds in the jazz guitar spectrum—as players like Joe Pass, Lenny Breau, Ron Escheté, and Tuck Andress have proved many times. While you can get by with conventional combo-type comping or a straight-four rhythm approach in contexts where there isn't a real bass player, walking bass lines add an entirely new dimension. (It's possible to play with a combination of pick and fingers, as well as fingers only.)

This type of comping differs in approach to solo pieces that incorporate melody, harmony, and a walking line where diverse elements and events require that you adhere to set fingerings—something more akin to playing a classical guitar piece than jazz. The style described here is designed to give the illusion of two or three parts occurring simultaneously, as you retain the freedom to vary your bass line at will, thereby avoiding monotonous repetition that can bore yourself, listeners, and the player you're supporting. As with practically everything associated with the guitar, there is almost no limit to the possibilities, although exactly how elaborately you can comp chords and play bass lines depends on a variety of factors, including tempo (the faster the piece, the less space there is to fill) and your own knowledge and ability.

As Joe Pass once said, "The most important aspect of playing chords and walking bass lines at the same time is the bass line itself." While bass lines vary in nature, overall you should think in terms of long, linear shapes that gracefully move up or down in register and then seamlessly reverse course. Once you understand and are able to achieve this concept to a degree, the next step is to add chords for harmonic support and rhythmic punctuation. Here's where a good knowledge of the easy-to-grab three-note chords described in Chapter 2 can be invaluable.

Constructing Walking Bass Lines

Since presenting bass lines in all common jazz keys could fill its own volume, all of the following examples are in G major, which provides easy access to these two common fingerboard landmarks: a sixth-string tonic (in G, the 3rd fret) and a fifth string tonic (at the 10th fret). Your initial goal should be to construct an effective walking bass line starting from each of these locations. Venturing above the fifth string, 10th fret, is common and often necessary. While the fifth-string area above the 5th fret overlaps the notes of the fourth string, confining your ideas to the 6th and 5th strings will not only maintain timbrel continuity in terms of the sound of the strings, but also force you into thinking more linearly, like a bass player who moves along the fingerboard rather than across it. That having been said, let's take a look at some bass lines.

In general, walking lines involve various combinations of two basic types of musical movement:
1. Linear motion that proceeds both diatonically and chromatically.
2. Widely variable skips that can include thirds-based and root-5th (arpeggio-related) activity.
These are illustrated in the following examples, which cover the first two measures, from I7 to IV7.

Bass Line Movement

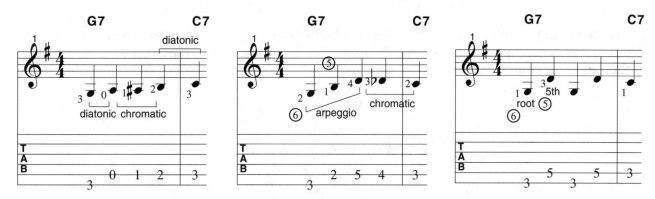

Roots & Approaches

To properly fulfill your function as a bass player, you need to play with great time and swing, delineate the chord changes, and vary your line and chord punctuations. Time and swing grow out of feel for and familiarity with the idiom, while playing with variety comes from experience. Delineating the changes relies on playing the right note at the right time, establishing musical landmarks as you go. More often than not these landmarks are the root of the chord at hand and occur on the first beat of the measure, although the remaining chord tones can also be used. (Rule: When two bars of a chord are featured, target the root for the downbeat of the first measure, reserving weaker-sounding notes like the 3rd or the 5th for the downbeat of the second bar.) With step-wise motion, a root generally can be approached in one of three ways: (1) from a half-step below, (2) from a scale step above (which may be either a half- or whole-step), and (3) from a half-step above. Thoroughly learn the following bass line so that playing it becomes second nature. Analyze how it outlines the chord changes, and especially notice the root connections. Fingerings are included, but remember that there are often several possibilities. Fingering takes on increasing importance when chords are added to the equation. A detailed description follows.

TRACK 24

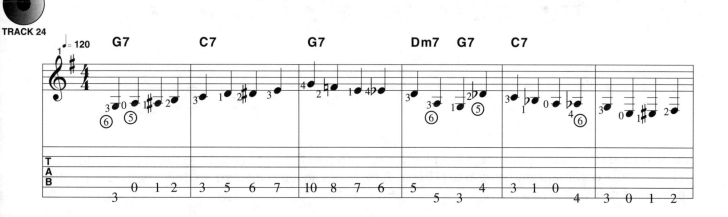

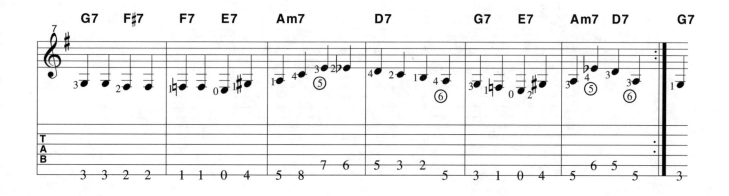

The preceding example begins on sixth-string G and walks up to fifth-string C. In measure 1, A♯ chromatically connects scale tones A and B, and bar 2's C is approached from a half-step below. Here's an alternative ascending walking line:

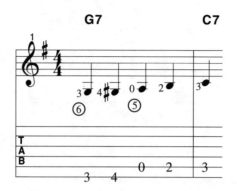

Measure 2 continues upward with the same idea, approaching bar 3's G by skip. In measure 3, the direction is reversed, leading to bar 4's Vm7-I7 (Dm7-G7, a IIm7-V7 of C) from a half-step above. Keep in mind that utilizing substitute chords can be useful in adding variety to areas where one chord is played for two or more measures. Measure 4 features root-5th movement (D to A), moves to G from a whole-step above, and then approaches bar 5's C from a half-step above. In the following examples, the first is a variation for measure 4's Vm7-I7 (it replaces G7 with D♭7, a ♭5 substitute), while the second possibility forgoes the II-V altogether (notice how it surrounds bar 5's C with notes that are a scale tone below, B, and a scale tone above, D):

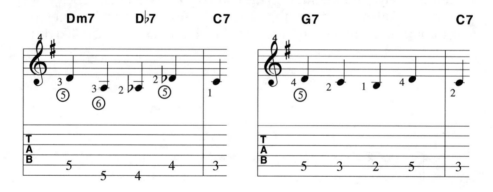

Measures 5 and 6 feature a hip line; bar 5 resolves to the 5th of C (G) in bar 6. Then the line skips down to E and walks chromatically upward to G in bar 7. Here's an an alternative route that targets G's 3rd (B) on bar 7's downbeat:

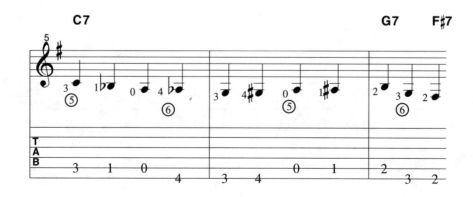

Your line needn't be in constant motion. In measures 7 and 8, the roots of G7, F#7, and F7 are all played twice, while bar 9's A root is approached from a half-step below. While there are several alternative progressions (chordal routes) for bars 7 and 8, they will be addressed in other parts of this section. Here are two common variations for this type of chromatic walk down:

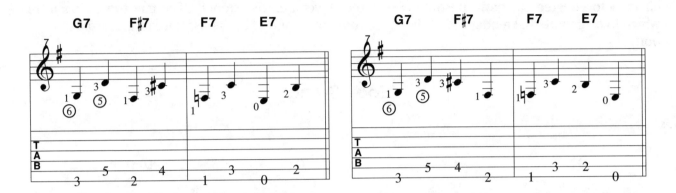

Measure 9 features an Am arpeggio (A-C-E) and chromatically descends to the root of bar 10's D. The line then walks down, purely by step, to the G root in measure 11. Bars 11 and 12 have a typical turnaround. Especially analyze whether the resolution to each chord's root moves up or down and if the approach is by a half- or a whole-step. There are many possible alternatives, several of which are covered later in this chapter. (Another alternative is playing bass lines in octaves.)

Chords & Walking Lines Together

This is the next step to being able to play bass lines and chords at the same time on the guitar. As mentioned earlier, chords reinforce the harmonic frame of reference and add rhythmic punch. Until playing walking bass lines becomes almost effortless, keep things simple. Chords can associated with the first beat of a measure, as in these examples—

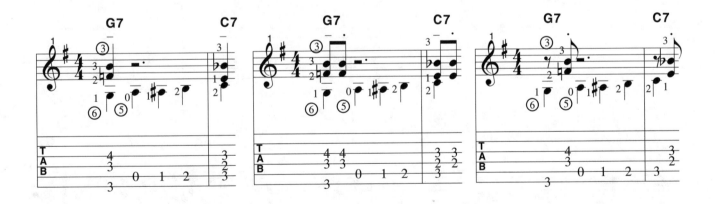

—or added elsewhere, as in examples to come. And it's good to be able to play any given chord with as many fingerings as possible.

The next example features a complete bass line that you should by now be familiar with. To keep things simple, it features chords played only on the "and" of beat one—with the exception of measures

4, 7, 8, 11, and 12, which feature two chords per measure and therefore include chords played on the "and" of beat three. Notice that fingering now takes on increased importance, enabling you to grab chords quickly, conveniently, and accurately while maintaining the bass line's flow.

The chords have a dual purpose: to enhance the sense of swing by providing rhythmic kicks and to help state the harmony more thoroughly; however, playing them in such a predictable manner, while effective to a degree, can grow tiresome to both the player and the listener. Of course, the main way in which to overcome that tendency is to increase your command of both bass lines and chordal punctuation.

"Joe's Swing"

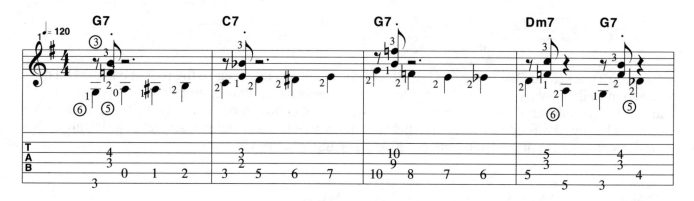

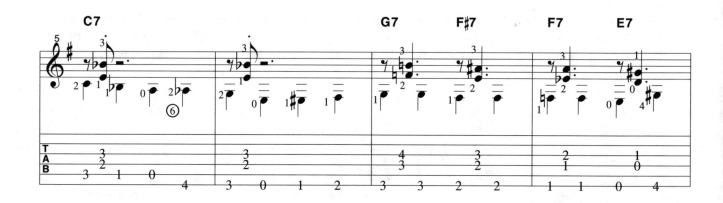

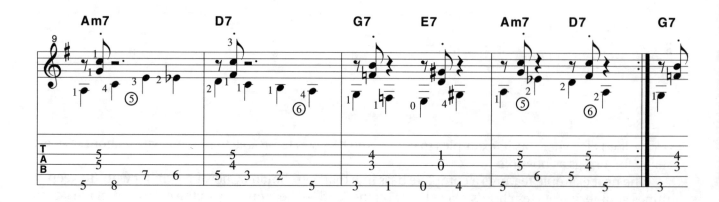

Increasing Rhythmic Variety—Chord Placement

Being able to vary where chords fall in relationship to the beat can mean the difference between an interesting, musical bass line and one that is stagnant. Even subtle changes can make a significant difference. To see how, first learn this bass line (it starts in a new geographical location, based on fifth-string G at the 10th fret; also try it, as well as the other lines in this chapter, in octaves.)—

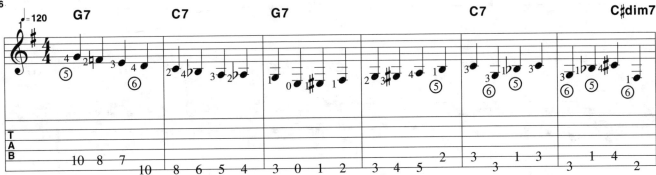

—and then take a look at the following example, which varies the relationship of the chords to beat one, placing them on the "and" of beat one like you've seen before, squarely on the beat as a quarter-note, and again on the beat but as a pair of eighths. The differences are subtle but effective.

"Soul Stroll"

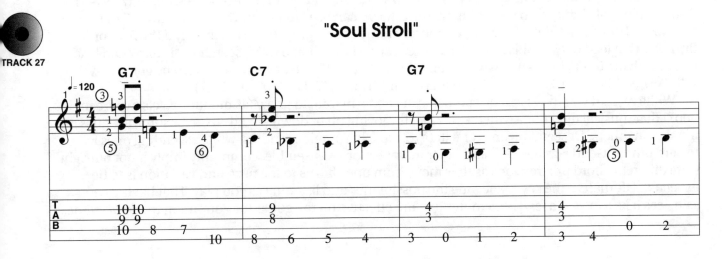

73

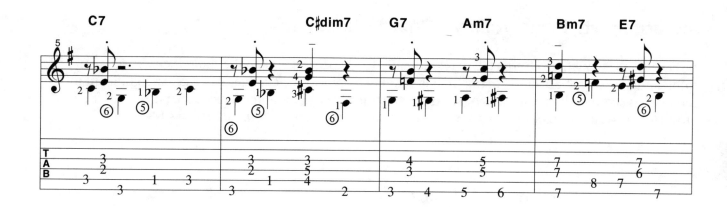

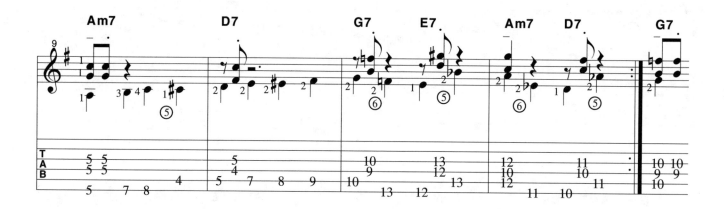

Before moving on, a few words about the preceding example. Notice the way the line descends in measures 1 and 2—a very common route. This time the chromatic line in bar 3 is applied to G7—you've seen it before, but for C7. Measure 5 features a cyclic type of idea that continues into the first half of bar 6, and is adapted to accommodate C♯dim7 leading to G7 in measure 7. Bars 7 and 8 progress similarly to "Stormy Monday." Measure 9 has a common minor walking line that continues upward through bar 10's D7. Finally, measures 11 and 12 feature a common turnaround. On your own, analyze how the first beat of every measure is approached.

Other Bass Line Routes

So far in looking at walking bass lines you've seen some minor deviations from the straight I7-IV7-VI7-IIm7-V7 types of changes. To review, in measure 4, you can use either a Vm7-I7 or a Vm7-♭V7 that resolves to IV7 (if you think of IV7 as a temporary tonic chord, or I7, these are merely a IIm7-V7 or a IIm7-♭II7 that lead to I7, in this case, C7). In the second half of bar 6 we've seen how ♯IVdim7 can lead to I7. In resolving to VI7 in bar 8, measure 7 and the first half of bar 8 have moved down by going I7-VII7-♭VII7-VI7 (G7-F♯7-F7-E7) or moved up with I7-IIm7-IIIm7-VI7 (G7-Am7-Bm7-E7).

While myriad variations can be confusing, it can be helpful to know (as mentioned elsewhere in this book) that musical direction—whether a voice is moving up or down—tends to favor some avenues more than others. Descending lines gravitate to some harmonic corridors, while ascending ones lean toward others. Good jazz bassists, and other members of an ensemble, commonly imply if not outright state different chord progressions as they move from one chorus to the next, and variation is to be expected. Ultimately, the key is knowing the possibilities and listening as you play. That having been said, let's take a look at a few more routes that are effective on the guitar (pay attention to the bass lines;

there are many possible chord voicings, and the rhythms have been intentional kept simple.).

Measure 1. Here the line starts out in one direction and then makes a sudden leap upward:

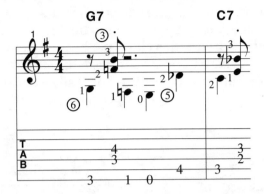

Measures 1 and 2. This avenue relies on repeated notes and is one of the most common bass clichés going. Although you'll find other keys that this works better in, it still sounds pretty good in this key and register. Here the very first chord is indicated as I7 (in this case, G), but you'll often find it stated as I6 (G6) or just plain I (G). In fact, the entire progression is most often indicated as I6-I7-IV7-IVm6-I. Bar 3 is given with the bass note only, since there are several chordal possibilities. Again, the most important aspect is the bass line.

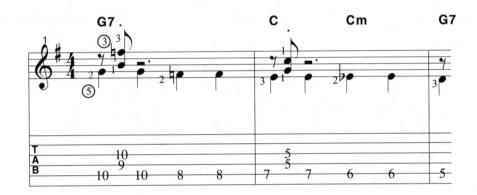

Measure 2. Three ways of connecting IV7 to I7 with ♯IVdim7. The first one features root-5th movement, while the second doubles the bass notes as it chromatically moves from the root of C7 up to the 5th of G7. Although IV7-♯IVdim7 naturally leads to a second-inversion I7, you can manipulate the line so that it takes you back to the root, as in the third example.

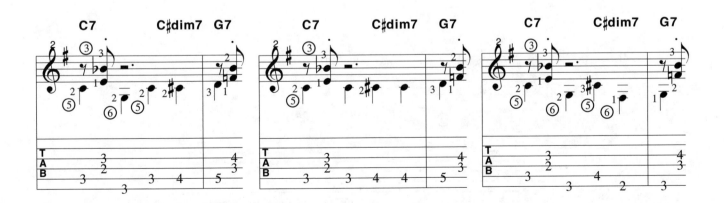

Measures 3 and 4. These next two examples use a series of chromatically descending chords. In the case of the first example, remember that there are any number of ways of getting into measure 4. (For an alternative bass route in measure 3, try playing a dominant 7th arpeggio: G, B, D, F, leading to bar 4's downbeat. Here measure 4 is harmonized with a chord per beat—essentially a short series of IIm7-♭II7's; however, it's possible to expand this chromatic sequence so that each chord lasts two beats, as in the second example, which begins on bar 3's downbeat and uses all minor 7th chords until two beats before C7.

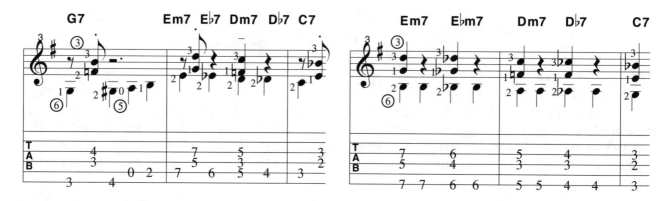

Measure 6. The "back door" approach—IVm7-♭VII7-I7— which is characteristic of so many bebop tunes:

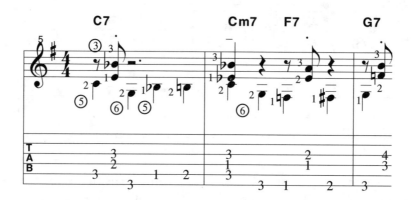

Measures 7 and 8. You've seen the basic idea before, but here the line is completely chromatic in bar 7 up to the first beat of measure 8, and then turns toward VI7 (you could continue the line upward to the root of VI7).

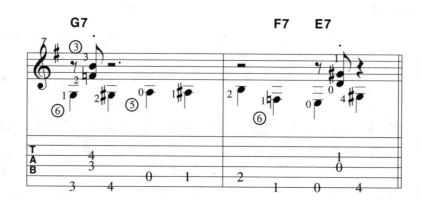

The progression beginning in bar 7—I7-IV7-IIIm7(or IIIm7♭5)-VI7—is associated with bebop. There are many ways you can get into measure 7 from bar 6; this is one possibility:

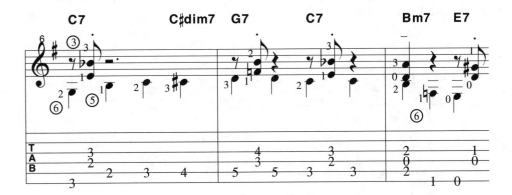

Here's the same progression, but the bass walks. Again, bar 6 is also included:

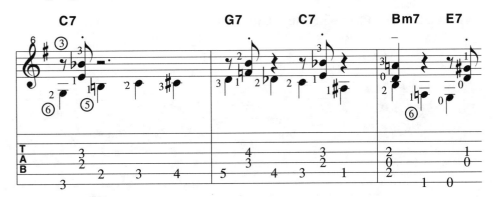

The same progression again, but in a different area of the fingerboard. Notice that this time it starts directly on bar 7:

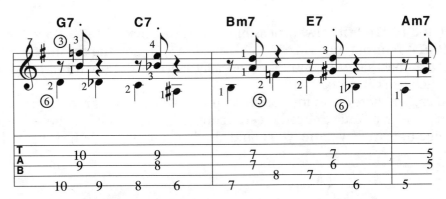

This one chromatically approaches VI7 like you've seen before, but from a different fingerboard perspective:

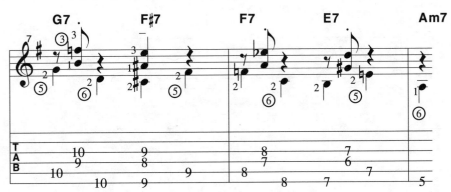

Measures 9 and 10. Keep in mind that II7 can always be used in place of IIm7. You've already seen a couple of the most common possibilities with IIm7-V7 in bars 9 and 10. This one descends from 6th-string A to low E, but then jumps up to D:

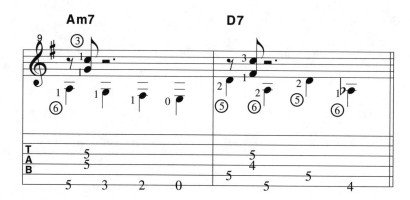

In a higher register, this one moves in a single direction:

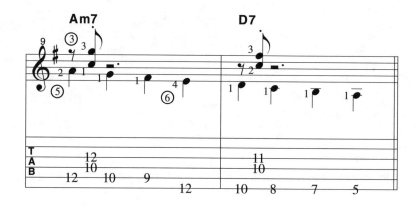

Measures 11 and 12. While it's always possible to use sequences like I7-♭IIImaj7-♭VImaj7-♭IImaj7 and IIIm7-VI7-IIm7-V7, turnarounds like I7-VI7-IIm7(or II7)-V7 and the chromatic I7-♭III7-II7-♭II7 sound bluesy. Remember that in a slow blues especially, you can also use turnarounds like the I-I7-IV6-IVm6-I-♭VI7-V7 shown in Chapter 2.

As mentioned earlier, there are many possible variations in terms of root approaches for walking through a I-VI-II-V pattern. You've already seen a couple. This one approaches each root from a half-step above and illustrates a new route (you could also begin it on the sixth string, 3rd fret):

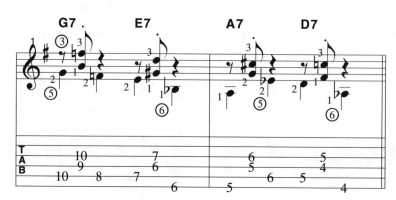

The chromatic I7-♭III7-II7-♭II7 turnaround works best when you double the bass notes, although there are other possibilities (on your own, work out variations in higher fingerboard positions):

Advanced Rhythms & Concepts

Now that you have a grasp of basic rhythms and are familiar with many of the chordal routes that walking bass lines can take, it's time to attend to more advanced matters—all of which will help you markedly vary your walking bass comping from chorus to chorus. The first topic concerns more advanced rhythms and how they apply to not only chords, but also to the bass lines themselves.

Fingering is often critical to playing additional rhythmic figures. The preceding examples primarily used short figures, usually associated with the first beat of the measure. You may have noticed, however, that in some cases, it was easy to sustain a chord beyond its notated time value because of its fingering and physical shape. By the same token, making slight but deliberate changes in the way you finger certain chords enables you to alter the length of their time value, which is an extremely valuable resource and something to keep in mind as you work through the upcoming material. For instance, fingering the following chords in the manner shown enables you to sustain them beyond just an eighth or quarter value:

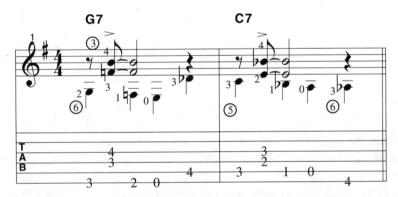

Anticipation. Anticipating a chord a half-beat before it's normally played results in a very hip sound—but it's often tricky to achieve and frequently requires careful fingering that can be hard to do on the spur of the moment. Nevertheless, the effect it creates is worth the effort. In this simple example, the conventional fingering limits the length of the notes:

With a few adjustments, though, the chords can be sustained for the entire measure, as in the following. Practically anything is possible, although, again, some rhythms and durations will be difficult to play spontaneously because they require so much preplanning.

Riff figures. Maintaining a consistent rhythmic figure throughout a 12-bar chorus can be extremely effective. Some rhythmic figures are easy to execute along with a walking bass line, as in the case of this example:

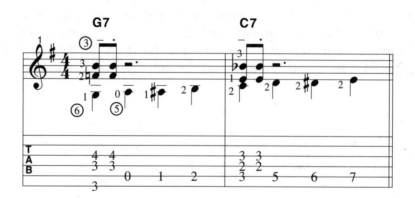

But certain figures can make things extremely difficult. This example features the same bass line as the preceding one, but its Charleston-like figure makes maintaining the bass and the chords quite a bit more problematic. Try maintaining the figure while playing a complete 12-bar walking bass line; write things out if necessary. You'll find the process enlightening and technically beneficial.

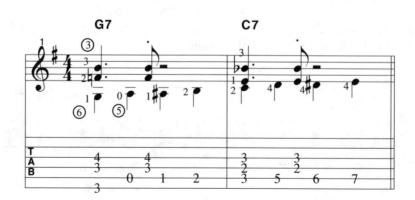

Quarter-note triplet (sometimes referred to as "super triplet") figures are also very hip-sounding, and especially work well for measures 7 and 8 and 11 and 12 of a 12-bar blues. To help you digest the rhythmic values, the following examples show the same passage notated in two different ways. The first example breaks each quarter-note triplet down into two eighth-note triplets, making things easier to count out, while the second example shows how the figure should really be notated. Carefully count these out so you can play them accurately, because they will be one of the hippest devices in your rhythmic vocabulary. You should also be able to invert the figure by playing the chords as straight quarter-notes and the bass notes as quarter-note triplets.

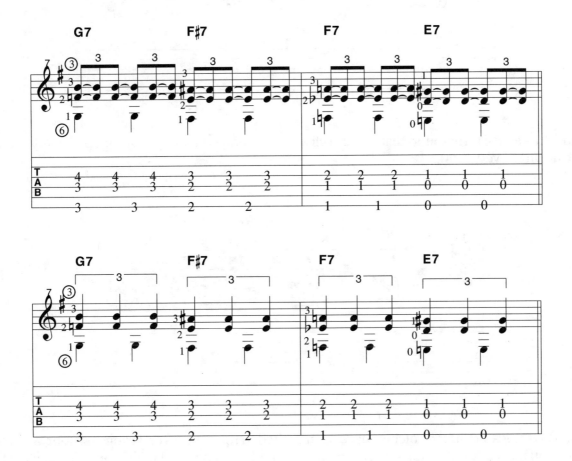

Using quarter-note triplets in different locations and in different ways can also be effective. Here, the first two beats of bar 1 include a quarter-note triplet figure:

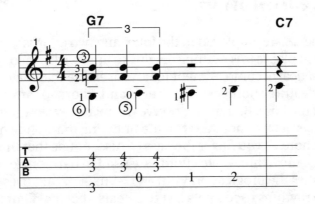

Bass line figures. Bass lines needn't always be made up of straight quarter-notes. There are many possibilities. In measure 1 of this example, notice how the root is doubled; beat four surrounds the upcoming C with a scale tone below an a scale tone above:

And here's a nice turnaround that works well at a slow tempo (also try moving up to every root, or moving down to every root):

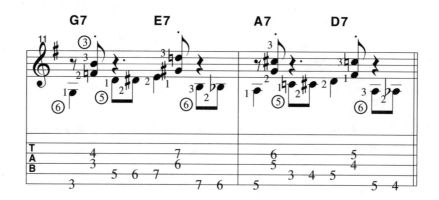

Chord Voicings. So far the voicings have been limited to three-notes on strings six, four, and three; however, you are really only limited to what you know and are capable of grabbing while juggling the bass line. The final example coming up gives a few possibilities.

Putting It All Together In G

Many of the preceding elements are employed in the following two choruses, which also include a variety of chord voicings. While in places this example begins to approach a solo guitar piece in complexity, it is designed to be a hypothetical accompaniment for an ensemble that includes at least one other instrument and might even feature another guitar, drums and a horn, or any combination of instruments with the exception of the bass. Be sure to observe the relatively slow tempo.

Measure 1 can be played exactly as notated with the fingering that's shown; however, you'll have to slightly cut short bar 2's C7 chord as you finger the bass G. Also, notice that the final G anticipates the upcoming downbeat. In measure 3 three-note chords are used to harmonize the bass line, which is covered in Chapter 2. Bar 4 implies the progression VIm7-♭VI7-Vm7-♭V7 and uses some common four-note voicings. Carefully learn the rhythms used for its last two beats; the final figure, a bass note followed by a chord on the second triplet eighth-note value, can be particularly effective.

Measures 5 through 8 employ a familiar bass line and use four-note voicings, which sound particularly good in 7 and 8 (observe the use of Bm7♭5). In bar 9, it's necessary to play C♯ with your 4th finger in order to sustain Am7 for its notated value. With the exception of the use of D9♯11 on the fourth beat, everything is fairly conventional in measure 10. Bar 12 briefly shifts to an ascending melodic line; beat four's bass is sacrificed in favor of a chordal figure that anticipates measure 13. Bar 13 also deviates from using a conventional walking bass and anticipates C13 on the "and" of beat four.

To hold C13 for its full time value in measure 14, keep fingers 2, 3 and 4 firmly planted as you reach for the B♭ at the 6th fret. Bars 15 through 18 feature more anticipations, some internal to the measure. (In bar 15, notice the repeated bass notes, which create a nice effect.) Measure 18 uses a IVm7-♭VII7 that resolves to 19's chromatic sequence with its quarter-note triplets.

Using a full barre in measure 21 will enable you to play the values as written. The bass line features root-5th movement. Bar 22 is relatively conventional and uses a bluesy V7♯9 chord, while the chromatic turnaround in measures 23 and 24 features anticipation throughout. Things conclude with a short, single-note tag.

"Totally Blue"

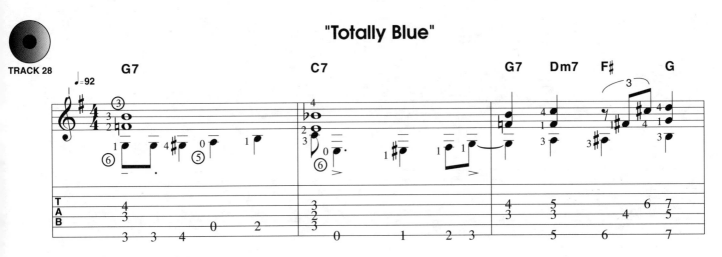

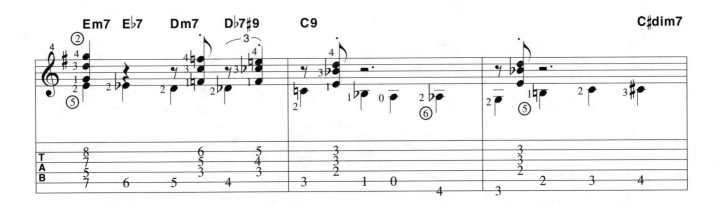

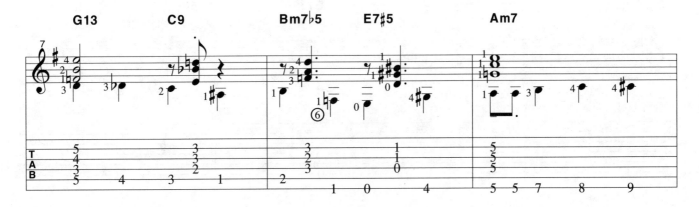

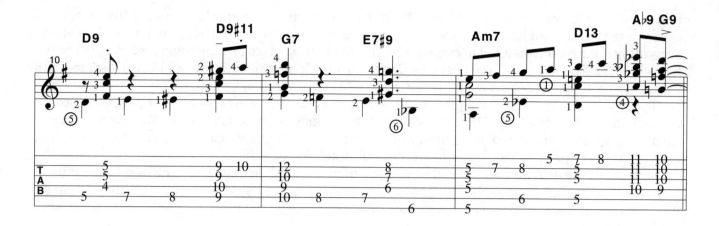

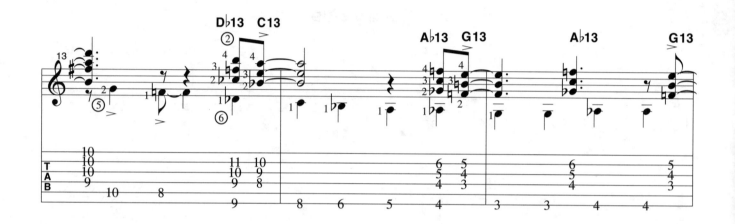

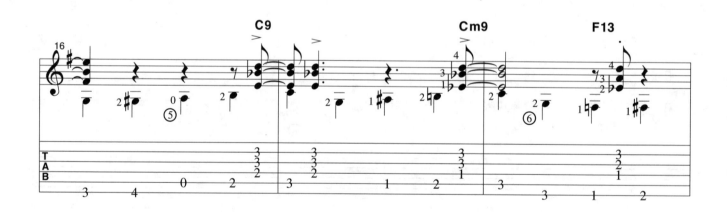

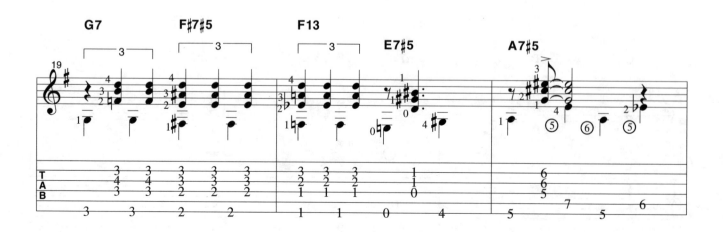

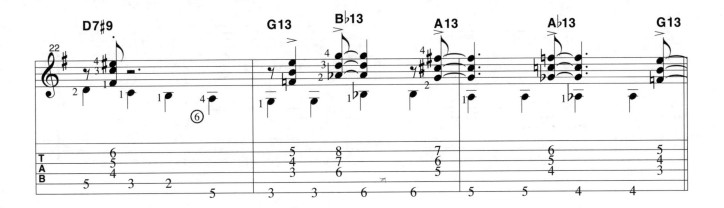

Bass Lines In Other Keys

Now that you have been introduced to a wide variety of bass lines, devices, and approaches, the next step is to apply these ideas to other "jazz" keys.

F Blues. This first line is in the key of F and works its way up from the sixth string, 1st fret, using a route seen earlier. Apply chords on your own.

TRACK 29

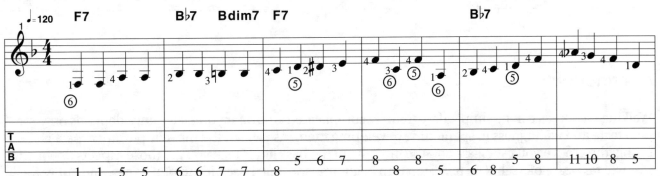

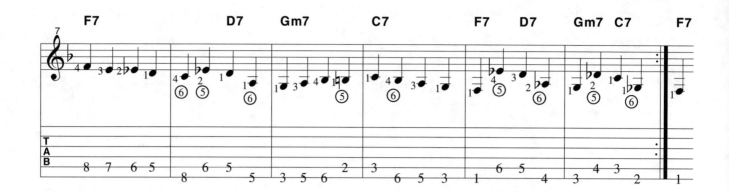

B♭ Blues. This line works it way down through an avenue traveled before, but begins in a lower register. Again, learn it on its own, and then apply chords.

TRACK 30

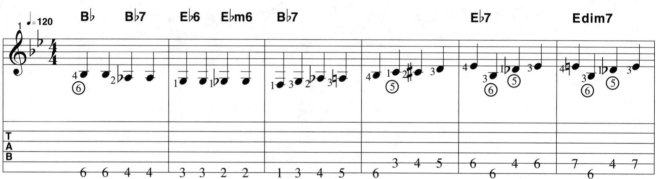

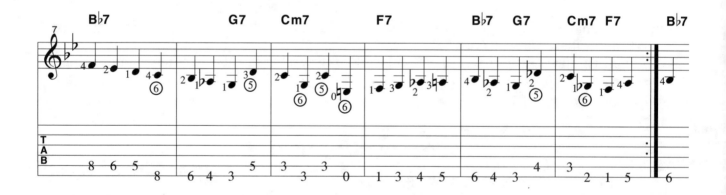

Afterthoughts

Walking bass lines can be simple or extremely complicated—how far you take things depends on your own taste and willingness to spend time developing them. As always, the most important aspect is swing, the groove you establish, and the integrity of the bass line. Once you get those aspects down, the rest will take care of itself. The next step is to begin transposing these idea to other keys, and apply the concepts to tunes other than 12-bar blues.

Glossary

The following list includes music- and guitar-related technical terms used in this book. For more information, consult a music dictionary

After beat—The second and fourth quarter-notes in a measure of 4/4. Normally thought to be weak, in jazz these are often the stressed beats. See *Back beat.*

Alteration—A chordal tone—usually the 5th, 9th, and 11th—that has been chromatically altered. The most common alterations are the ♭5, ♯5, ♭9, ♯9, and ♯11.

Anticipation—Playing a note, melodic idea, or chord before it would normally occur in relationship to the beat. Anticipations often occur a half-beat earlier than usual.

Arpeggio—The notes of a chord played one at a time, not necessarily in order. Arpeggios are often referred to as broken or rolled chords.

Articulation—How a note is attacked or sounded. Articulation and phrasing are closely associated.

Back beat—The second and fourth quarter-notes in a measure of 4/4. Normally thought to be weak, in jazz these are often the stressed beats. See *After beat.*

Barre—A guitar technique in which a left-hand finger—usually the 1st—is held rigid and/or slightly curved, enabling it to depress two or more strings simultaneously at the same fret.

Block chord—On the guitar, a fixed left-hand chord fingering that usually involves at least four notes.

Blues scale—The minor pentatonic scale (root, ♭3, 4, 5, ♭7) with the ♭5/♯4 added.

Chart—A form of sheet music used in jazz and popular music. Charts can come in more than one form. Lead sheets include a song's melody and chord changes, while a chord chart includes merely the chord changes and the number of measures.

Chord quality—A term referring to whether a chord is major, minor, augmented, diminished, or dominant. Within each category, it is possible to describe even more specific characteristics (i.e., whether a chord is a 9th, 11th, etc.).

Chorus—In jazz parlance, one complete time through a song's form. Also, an improvised solo that lasts for one complete time through a song's form.

Chromatic—In general, half-step movement. (Although, technically, in contrast to diatonic half-step movement where two consecutive notes have different letter names and therefore appear on different lines and spaces, as in B-C, chromatic movement involves consecutive notes in the same space or on the same line and therefore the notes in question have the same letter name, as in G-G♯). See *Diatonic.*

Chord scale—A scale where each note is supported by a harmonic structure.

Circle of fifths—Also known as the cycle of fifths or "the wheel," it is the clockwise arrangement of successive keys in ascending fifths: C, G, D, A, E, B (C♭), F♯ (G♭), C♯(D♭), A♭, E♭, B♭, F. Many jazz progressions normally move through this sequence in reverse order, as in Em7-A7-Dm7-G7, etc.

Clave figure—A rhythmic figure used in Latin music, so called because it is often played with the claves, a percussion instrument consisting of two cylindrical pieces of wood.

Close voicing—Traditionally, a chord whose upper- and lowermost notes fall within one octave. Also, a structure that includes one or more second intervals.

Common tone—A note found in the same voice of two or more successive chords. Common tones are most often featured in the upper voice, but can also be internal to or the lowest member of a series of harmonic structures.

Comping—Accompanying, supporting, or backing up an instrumentalist or vocalist in a way that normally features chords and steady rhythm. The term is sometimes thought to derive from the word complement.

Contrary motion—Two voices moving in opposite directions. See *Similar motion* and *Voice.*

Counter riff—A riff that moves counter to or contrasts with a primary riff. See *Riff* and *Secondary riff.*

Damp—On the guitar, to intentionally muffle or deaden a string so that it will not produce a discernible pitch if played.

Degree—A scale tone or note.

Diatonic—Scale movement in which two successive notes move in either a whole- or half-step relationship and advance from a line to a space (or vice versa) up or down and therefore have different letter names. See *Chromatic.*

Double stop—Two notes played at the same time on the same instrument.

Downbeat—The first beat of a measure.

Downstroke—Sounding a string with a motion directed toward the floor. See *Upstroke.*

Enharmonic—Notes that sound the same but are spelled differently are said to be enharmonic. All (but one) notes have three different possible names, made possible by the use of the flat, the sharp, the double flat and the double sharp. Chords can also be enharmonic.

Extension—Unaltered chordal tones encompassing the 9th, 11th, and 13th. Extensions are sometimes referred to as tensions. See *Alteration.*

Fake book—A collection of charts to common jazz songs. See *Chart.*

Fall—An articulation common to jazz in which a given pitch is sounded and then allowed to descend rapidly. Falls usually last approximately two beats. The individual pitches may or may not be discernible, depending on the type of fall required.

First inversion—An arrangement of the notes of a chord in which the 3rd is the lowest member. See *Root position, Second inversion,* and *Third Inversion.*

Form—The overall structure of a song in terms of its number of measures and sections.

Guide finger—A guitar technique in which a left-hand finger remains in contact with a string to facilitate a position change.

Head—The melody of a song.

Hi-hat—A component of a drum set involving a pair of horizontally mounted cymbals operated by a foot pedal.

Inversion—An arrangement of the notes of a chord or scale in which the lowest pitch is a chordal tone other than the tonic, or root. See *First inversion, Second inversion, Third inversion,* and *Mode.*

Inversion-specific—A term in this book that refers to a progression that is dependent upon chords whose notes are in specific arrangements, including root position, first inversion, and second inversion.

Lick—A memorized phrase applied in an improvisational context. See *Riff.*

Modal—Music whose pitches and harmonic structures derive from a particular mode or modes. See *Mode.*

Mixolydian mode—The fifth mode of the major scale. In relationship to the major scale, the Mixolydian mode is spelled root, 2, 3, 4, 5, 6, ♭7. See *Mode.*

Mode—The inversions of a diatonic scale. The seven modes of the major scale are Ionian, Dorian, Phrygian, Lydian, Mixolydian, Aeolian, and Locrian. See *Diatonic* and *Inversion.*

Motive—A short melodic or rhythmic idea. Also known as a motif, germ, or cell.

Octave—Two pitches of the same name separated by 12 half-steps.

Off the beat—A point in time halfway between two successive beats. See *On the beat.*

On the beat—A point in time that precisely coincides with the occurrence of a beat. See *Off the beat.*

Open voicing—A chord whose upper- and lowermost notes exceed the distance of one octave.

Ostinato—A repeated melodic and/or rhythmic motive. See *Motive.*

Passing chord—A chord used for the purpose of generating movement and possibly connecting two principle harmonies. Passing chords can be diatonic, chromatic, or employ properties of each. See *Chromatic* and *Diatonic.*

Phrase—A complete melodic or rhythmic idea. Phrases are normally from one to four measures long.

Pickup—A melodic element as short as a single note that leads into the first complete measure of a song.

Progression—A series of chords. Progressions can constitute short patterns or entire songs.

Resolution—A chordal close or resting point.

Rhythm changes—A common 32-bar jazz vehicle, so called because it is based on the chords to Gershwin's "I Got Rhythm."

Riff—A distinctive, often short phrase that is repeated for the purpose of building tension or providing a kind of accompanying motif. See *Lick.*

Roman numeral symbolization—A method of indicating basic chordal root movement independent of key. While there are several Roman numeral systems currently in use, in this book, the notes of the major scale are indicated with Roman numerals accompanied by letters and numbers that reflect the quality of a certain chord. Roman numerals reflecting a major scale diatonically harmonized in 7th chords would be Imaj7, IIm7, IIIm7, IVmaj7, V7, VIm7, VIIm7♭5. Deviations from the basic diatonic Roman numerals can be indicated by applying accidentals, as in IVm7-♭VII7-I.

Root—The note from which a chord or scale derives its name. Also known as the tonic or fundamental. See *Tonic.*

Root position—A chord in which the note from which it derives its name occupies the lowest position or bass voice.

Score—Notated music; sheet music.

Secondary riff—A riff of secondary importance to a main riff. See *Riff* and *Counter riff.*

Second inversion—An arrangement of the notes of a chord in which the 5th is the lowest member. See *Root position, First inversion,* and *Third inversion.*

Shout chorus—A spirited, climactic, often riff-based chorus associated with big bands.

Shuffle—A blues-based rhythm associated with a swing-eighths feel.

Similar motion—Two voices moving in the same general musical direction. See *Contrary motion* and *Voice.*

Slash chord—A chord symbol that includes a slash and a letter to the right of the slash indicating a specific bass note (i.e., Am/G). Slash chords and triads over bass notes are similar; however, the bass notes of slash chords are usually chordal tones and therefore do not constitute a novel harmonic structure. See *Triads over bass notes.*

Stepwise movement—Movement that progresses diatonically. See *Diatonic.*

Straight four—Slang for a swing rhythm guitar approach in which a chord is played per beat. Sometimes known as "four on the floor."

Substitute—A chord or set of chords used to replace a conventional harmony or harmonies. Substitute chords can merely embellish an existing progression, or dramatically and creatively transform a familiar song into something new.

Swing—A jazz period generally defined as the years 1935 to 1946; music relying on repetitive, riff-based melodic and rhythmic patterns and frequently bluesy melodies.

Synonym—An alternative name (and therefore possible use) for a harmonic structure. All harmonic structures can be applied in more than one way.

Tablature—An alternative notational system designed for string instruments. In conventional guitar tablature, six lines represent the instrument's six strings, with the top line representing the first, or highest sounding, string. Positioned on the lines are numbers, which indicate the fret at which a given string is to be played. A "0" indicates an open, or unfretted, string, a "1" represents the first fret, a "2" the second, and so on.

Third inversion—An arrangement of the notes of a chord in which the 7th is the lowest member. See *Root position, First inversion,* and *Second inversion.*

Tonic—The note from which a chord or scale derives its name. Also known as the root or fundamental. See *Root.*

Transformation—A term coined by Howard Roberts that describes how a note of a harmonic structure can be changed to generate a new, albeit frequently related, structure. For example, the 6th of C6 can be raised to produce C7.

Triad—The simplest complete harmonic structure. Triads have three notes: a root (or tonic), a 3rd, and a 5th. There are four qualities of triads: major, minor, augmented, and diminished.

Triads over bass notes—A technique for generating often unorthodox harmonic structures whereby a triad is voiced above a bass note. Some bass notes merely double notes of the triad, while others not normally associated with the triad can result in novel structures. See *Slash chord* and *Triad.*

Turnaround—Often the last two measures of a song, usually neutral melodic ground where a number of harmonic devices can be applied, including a series of chords leading back to the first measure.

Upstroke—Sounding a string or strings with an upward motion that moves away from the floor.

Voice—A chordal tone or a line in a series of harmonies.

Voice-leading—The act of smoothly connecting voices from one chord to the next. See *Voice.*

Voicing—The arrangement of notes in a chord.

Other books by Jim Ferguson

Jim Ferguson and Guitar Master Class are devoted to producing innovative books that are designed to help you play better, faster.

"Ferguson's [first three] books are essential for anyone wishing to expand their jazz vocabulary."—Jimmy Bruno

"Essential for all of my students." —Howard Morgen

"Superb. One of the most comprehensive and clearly presented approaches to this much dissected subject."—20th Century Guitar

"Taken together, [Ferguson's books] offer myriad options in navigating various blues forms. An essential resource for students."—JazzTimes

NOTES